Let's Explore the Beach!

Let's Explore the Beach!

A Young Naturalist's Guide to Pacific Coastal Wildlife

Karen DeWitz

little bigfoot
an imprint of sasquatch books
seattle, wa

When you know to look, you see.

When you see, you get excited.

When you're excited, you care.

Young or old, this book is for those ready to look.

Manufactured in China by C&C Offset Printing Co. Ltd. Shenzhen, Guangdong Province, in October 2023

LITTLE BIGFOOT with colophon is a registered trademark of Penguin Random House LLC

28 27 26 25 24   9 8 7 6 5 4 3 2 1

Editors: Michelle McCann and Christy Cox
Production editor: Isabella Hardie
Designer: Tony Ong
Interior photographs:
    Plankton photo (page 25): ©tonaquatic / Adobe Stock
    Sea otter photographs (pages vii, 122–123): Taken by Karen DeWitz at the Seattle Aquarium

Library of Congress Cataloging-in-Publication Data is available.

ISBN: 978-1-63217-442-0

Sasquatch Books
1325 Fourth Avenue, Suite 1025
Seattle, WA 98101

SasquatchBooks.com

FSC
www.fsc.org

MIX
Paper | Supporting
responsible forestry
FSC® C008047

Contents

Welcome to the Pacific Coast!

There is so much to discover here if you know where to look. The Pacific coastline is home to tens of thousands of different species of marine plants and animals. Some of these creatures have been around since before the dinosaurs. There are signs of life everywhere, and learning about them makes the beach a new adventure every time you go.

From otters to pelicans, the Pacific coast is filled with creatures living their fascinating lives right out in plain sight.

How to Use This Book

This guide is written to help young naturalists—and anyone else curious about the amazing wildlife along the Pacific coast—know what to look for while wandering the shore. Does it cover everything you might come across? Wonderfully, no! (But it definitely covers a lot.) You'll start to see new things you've never noticed before once you really start looking. What a great reason to keep going back to the beach!

The book is divided into three parts: tide pools, shoreline, and shorebirds. There's lots of overlap in the real world, but in this book each section highlights a different collection of Pacific coastal life and other cool treasures. You will learn about a variety of animals, seaweed, and interesting nonliving finds along the Pacific coast. For each *living* entry, there are six types of information:

NAME: What is it called?

APPEARANCE: What does it look like?

FOOD: What does it eat, and/or what eats it?

HABITAT: What kind of environment does it like?

REPRODUCTION: Does it have babies, lay or release eggs, or just clone itself?

RANGE: Where does it live?

There will also be hints to help you find and appreciate treasures like agates, shells, and fossils as you wander the shore.

Thor's Well—Yachats, Oregon

The Ocean

To get the most out of a trip to the coast, start by thinking about its biggest giant: the Pacific Ocean—a single body of water that covers almost a third of the earth's surface. The Pacific is bigger than all of the land of all the continents on Earth put together. It has deep places that humans haven't explored and life forms people have never seen. A trip to the Pacific coast puts you on the edge of that huge, unknown mystery. The wind, waves, and wildlife are constantly changing. No matter how many times you go back to the same beach, you may find something new with each visit.

Tides

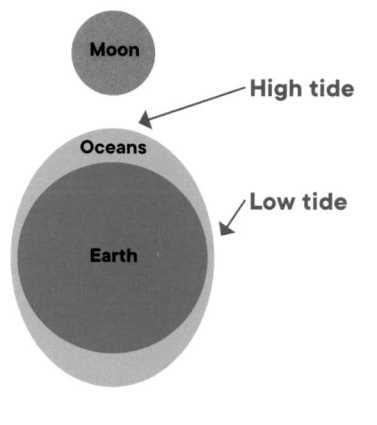

All day and night, waves crash on the shore. Over the course of about 6 hours, they reach higher and higher up the beach, covering everything in water. At high tide, the waves are as far up the beach as they're going to go. Then they start crashing farther and farther out for the next 6 hours. The point where the waves are the farthest out from the shore is called low tide. This cycle happens twice a day—two high tides and two low tides.

Why does this happen? Believe it or not, the tides rise and fall because of the sun and the moon! The gravity of the sun and the moon (mostly the moon) pulls on the earth. Since water is easier to move than rock, the land keeps its shape while the water in the oceans bulges on opposite sides of the globe. As the planet rotates under those bulges, the water gets deeper and then shallower in different places. When a spot on the earth is under one of the bulges, it's high tide there. In the graphic above, that would be the spots at the very top and bottom of

Wrack line

the globe. When that spot rotates to the shallower part of the water (not under a bulge), it's low tide. In the graphic above, that would be the spots on both sides of the globe. When the sun and moon line up and pull together, you get super high and low tides—and a super time to check out the beach!

Low tide is when the water pulls back to reveal hidden tide pools, shells, and sea treasures washed up on the wrack line (or wrack zone). That's the line of seaweed, shells, and other floating stuff that gets left on the beach at the edge of the highest tide. Don't just walk by! This is a great place to look for signs of life.

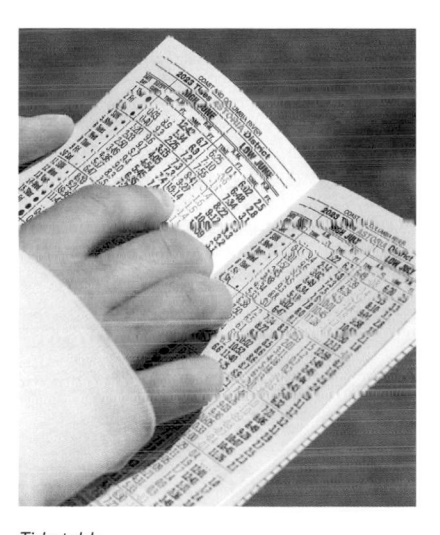

Tide table

You can find out when high and low tides will be ahead of your beach trip. Do an internet search for the area you're visiting and include the words "tide chart" (or "tide table"). The chart will show you the high and low tides in that area by date and time. You can also

pick up a tide table booklet in local shops or visitors' centers for the areas you're visiting. Look on the chart for the letters *H* labeling high tide and *L* labeling low tide, which includes the approximate time of day the tides occur. You will also see a number: the lower the number at low tide, the farther out the water will be. Some low tides are even labeled with *negative* numbers. Those are called minus tides, and that means the tide will be extra far out. Minus tides are great times to hunt for unusual beach life!

Along with super-low minus tides, the coast can also have extra-high "king tides." Those sometimes happen during a new or full moon. They can be amazing to watch, but be especially careful when tides are extra high. King tides can make the beach unsafe even for experienced explorers. Giant waves can crash way up on the sand without warning, sometimes flooding roads and surrounding areas. Plan ahead and pay attention to high and low tides to have the best and safest time exploring along the shore.

Intertidal life splashed by
the surf

Sea anemone   Ocean-hunting river otter with a snack

Intertidal Zones

The area on the beach between the low tide point and the high tide point is called the intertidal zone. The animals and plants that live there have adapted (changed their bodies or behaviors over time) to survive pounding waves, high wind, and time spent both underwater and out in the dry air. The intertidal zone is where curious beachgoers will find the most amazing coastal treasures, including tide pools, stretches of life-filled sand and rocks, and many of the birds described in this book.

Ochre sea stars (Pisaster ochraceus)

Animal Names

Naming things you see in the wild should be simple, right? You know what different creatures are called: otter, crab, fish, bird. What could be easier? It's more complicated than you might think, though. What specific type of fish is this? Which species of bird is that? To answer these questions, we use different kinds of names and labels.

First, there's the common name. That's the label most people use. For example, if you see an orange star-shaped creature on the beach, you might call it a starfish. But others might call that same animal a

Purple sea urchins (Strongylocentrotus purpuratus), a white urchin test, an orange sea cucumber (Cucumaria miniata), and seaweed

Gooseneck barnacles (Pollicipes polymerus), ochre sea stars (Pisaster ochraceus), California mussels (Mytilus californianus), and aggregating anemones (Anthopleura elegantissima)

purple star, a common sea star, an ochre sea star, an ochre starfish, or a warty sea star. (Whew!) In other cases, lots of different individual species may share a common name. A "snail" might refer to anything from a tiny periwinkle to a giant moon snail. How do scientists and naturalists (nature experts) keep them straight?

Pygmy rock crab (Glebocarcinus oregonensis), a crustacean that is also a decapod

Scientists sort plants and animals into groups that have something in common. Many marine animals, such as crabs and shrimp, have a hard outer shell, so they are in a big group called crustaceans (pronounced crus-TAY-shuns). Those same animals belong to other groups as well. For example, both crabs and shrimp have ten legs, so they are also in a group called decapods (which means "ten legs or feet"). They both also lay eggs, so they are in the big group of egg-laying (oviparous) animals. In this book, you'll learn several of these group names. They can help naturalists (including you!) think about how different animals are similar.

To be absolutely clear about which plant or animal they're describing, researchers also use scientific names. Every known species on Earth has a two-part scientific name that applies to only that specific plant or animal. The first word in the name is capitalized; the second word isn't. Also, the scientific name is written in italics, or slanted text. The scientific name for the pygmy rock crab (above), for example, is *Glebocarcinous oregonensis*. Scientific names can be a mouthful!

In this book, you'll see common names as well as scientific names (in parentheses after the common name). Choose whichever way of identifying beach life appeals to you.

A Beachcomber's Pledge

I promise to . . .

- Look before I step. Lots of rocks and watery pools are covered with beach life. I will be careful to keep my feet on sand and bare rock.

- Think about how my actions will affect the wildlife. Am I hurting an animal? Did I scare away its lunch? Did I move a creature into another animal's territory?

- Use just one or two clean wet fingers to gently touch fragile tide pool creatures. I am a giant compared to them, so I will keep my actions extra light while exploring. I will also keep chemicals like lotion and sunscreen out of beach ecosystems, which can be more sensitive to products than I am.

- Remember that every action I take is multiplied by the number of people who go there before and after me. It's not just me; it's millions of me.

- Always respect the ocean. I won't turn my back on the waves or climb anywhere water might cut me off from the shore. I will always be ready to move to a safer location.

- Leave the beach even better than I found it. I will haul out my trash and pick up any garbage I find along the shore.

Tide Pools

Tucked into small pools of salt water at the base of rocky shores, you can explore creatures that seem like they're straight out of science fiction. Some look like flowers stuck on the end of fat elephant trunks. Others spend their adult lives glued facedown on rocks, grabbing food with their legs. Tide pools let you investigate creatures and plants that are unlike anything you've ever seen on land.

At low tide, these natural aquariums will be out of the surf, where you can reach them. Serious tide pool explorers (or "tide poolers") wear rubber boots or comfortable water shoes to get to the most interesting areas. It's always best not to go barefoot—you never know when you might step on a sharp shell or disturb something with pincers or stinging tentacles. Move slowly, look carefully, and prepare to be amazed!

Anemone, Sea

Sea anemones (pronounced uh-NEM-uh-nees) are some of the most interesting and beautiful creatures you'll find along the Pacific coast. They're often attached to rocks in and around tide pools, held in place by their one big sticky foot. Can they move around? Some can, but the movement is usually too slow to see. They tend to mostly stay put.

Aggregating anemones

The tentacles surrounding an anemone's mouth contain stinging cells called nematocysts (pronounced NEH-ma-te-sists). Those stinging cells can stun small prey but aren't strong enough to puncture human skin. That means you can gently touch the tentacles of a sea anemone in the water, and all you'll feel is a sticky grabbing sensation as it curves around your finger. Give it a try! Remember that these are animals, though, and be gentle.

When they're out of the water at low tide, anemones look completely different from their underwater selves. They pull their tentacles in toward their bodies to keep from drying out. They don't have bones or shells, but many anemones do have sticky bumps on their outsides that collect small rocks and shells for camouflage and protection.

Along the Pacific coast, different species of sea anemones range from tiny—less than ¼ inch—to over 11 inches across at the tentacles.

Aggregating Anemone

(Anthopleura elegantissima)

The aggregating anemone is one of the most common species of anemone found on the Pacific coast. But common doesn't mean boring!

APPEARANCE: These anemones are fairly small, ranging from ½ inch to as large as 3 inches across. But what they lack in individual size, they make up for in numbers. The word *aggregating* in their name means "forming into a cluster or group." You can find them in large groups blanketing the rocks around tide pools. Aggregating anemones are usually greenish with pink on the tips of their tentacles.

FOOD: Aggregating anemones are carnivores, which means they're animals that eat meat. They don't move around to hunt their prey, though.

Aggregating anemones covering a rock out of the water at low tide. Careful, those blobs are alive!

Check out these beauties! A few near the bottom of this photo are closed, but those at the top are open. Can you spot a mouth in the middle of each ring of tentacles? The anemone near the center has three blobs near its mouth that look like shells. Those

are part of the inside of its body cavity called the pharynx (pronounced FARE-inks), which is kind of like its throat. The anemone sometimes pushes its pharynx out through its mouth while it feeds!

Instead, they wait for the tide to wash small creatures like isopods (see page 114) and amphipods (see page 102) past their grabbing tentacles. After an anemone stings its prey, its tentacles pull the food toward its mouth in the very center of the "flower." Once the prey goes through the mouth into the tubelike body, the anemone digests what it can. Then, because it only has the one opening, whatever food can't be digested comes back out through the mouth hole. If you look carefully, you can often see shells and other undigestible bits clustered around an anemone's mouth.

This anemone is dividing in half to form two animals out of one.

See those white tips at the ends of the outside tentacles? This aggregating anemone is ready for battle.

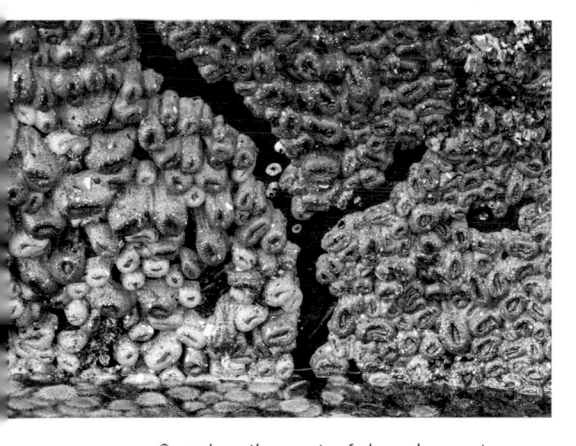

See where these sets of clones have set up no-go zones? What differences can you spot between the anemones on the left and on the right? These are all aggregating anemones, but each group of clones has a slightly different look.

HABITAT: These anemones live in and around tide pools and on exposed rocks in the intertidal zone.

REPRODUCTION: To make more of themselves, aggregating anemones can spray eggs into the surf, or they can clone themselves by splitting in half to form a new, identical animal. Every clone is an exact copy of the anemone it came from. Clones will all happily crowd together (aggregate) on a rock or pier, but when they meet up with clones of another individual, they'll have a turf war! The anemones at the edges of two different groups of clones fight each other with special white stinging tentacles. Those battles eventually leave little "do not cross" pathways along the rocks dividing groups of clones.

RANGE: Common from Alaska down to Baja California, Mexico.

Who knew? When they're underwater, anemones can look like flowers. In fact, their common name comes from a colorful land flower also called an anemone. The "petals" on the sea version are actually tentacles surrounding an oral disc—like the center of a flower, but with a mouth in the middle.

Anemone flower

Giant Green Anemone
(Anthopleura xanthogrammica)

Like their name suggests, these anemones are big and green. In fact, they're the largest anemones on the Pacific coast. These green giants can live around 80 years in the wild but have been kept alive for up to 150 years in captivity.

APPEARANCE: Giant green anemones can grow to over 11 inches across at the tentacles. Those short tentacles are usually a brighter green than their body. Their thick, tubelike bodies are olive green, bumpy, and can be up to 11 inches long. These creatures sometimes look like short, droopy elephant trunks when they're out of the water (see photo on page 204). The giant green is also one of the anemones with sticky bumps that it uses to hold small rocks and shells to its body for protection.

FOOD: Giant green anemones eat small fish, shrimp, crabs, urchins, and other similar prey that they grab with their tentacles and pull into their mouth.

HABITAT: These animals can be found in tide pools and on rocks where the ocean water will be splashing and surging. They are found alone and in groups.

REPRODUCTION: This animal releases eggs into the water, where they hatch into larvae—kind of like how butterflies start out as caterpillars. These larvae don't look anything like caterpillars, though. They go through several stages where they look more like microscopic (tiny), see-through, upside-down octopuses. The larvae eventually settle down and transform into small versions of adult anemones.

RANGE: Common all the way from Alaska down to Central America.

Other Species to Look For

MOONGLOW ANEMONE

(Anthopleura artemisia)

This beautiful species can be a wide range of colors, from pink or blue to green or brown. Look for white bands across the tentacles to help identify this one.

PAINTED ANEMONE (*Urticina crassicornis*)

This anemone has a column that often has patches of red and green, so some people call it a Christmas anemone.

STUBBY ROSE ANEMONE (*Urticina coriacea*)

This anemone usually has short, stubby tentacles and a deep brick-reddish column.

Who knew? Giant green and aggregating anemones have a secret hiding inside them: it's algae (pronounced AL-jee). Algae are plantlike organisms that, like green plants on land, can make sugar from sunlight. Some anemones have algae living right inside their cells! This is called a symbiotic relationship, where different life forms live closely together (even *in* each other) and everyone gets something from the deal. In this case, the algae are protected from animals that might eat them, and their anemone home can turn and bend to catch the sunlight. In exchange, the anemones get extra energy and nutrients from the algae. Everybody wins!

Barnacle

Barnacles (pronounced BAR-nuh-culls) are some of the toughest creatures on the coast. They spend time underwater in the cold ocean, but they can also survive longer than most other intertidal creatures out in the sun. If you look at rocks and cliffs, you can often see barnacles well above where all the other sea life stops.

They may look like part of the rocks they live on, but barnacles are actually a type of crustacean, which means "having a crust or shell." Crabs and shrimp are some other crustaceans you may have seen.

Gooseneck barnacles

Who knew? After they hatch, baby barnacles drift around in the water as larvae (like a lot of other sea creatures). After about six months, they attach themselves headfirst to a hard surface around other barnacles. And once they're in place, they never move again. It's a lifelong headstand! The glue they make for this is so strong that scientists are studying it to see if we can copy or collect it for human use.

Barnacle cirri molt   *Acorn and thatched barnacles*

As adults, barnacles build themselves a hard shell made out of overlapping plates. They use their feathery legs—called cirri—to sweep through the water and bring food inside their shell to their mouth. As they grow, barnacles shed the shells on their cirri when they outgrow them. This process is called molting, and the cast-off shell is called a molt. When you explore the wrack line along the sand, you can sometimes find the cast-off molts of barnacle cirri.

Barnacles don't have a heart or lungs, but they still have blood and need oxygen. Instead of a heart, their blood is pumped through their bodies by other muscles. They "breathe" though their body walls and cirri.

There are more than 1,400 barnacle species found all over the world. Two of the most common types seen along the Pacific coast are acorn and gooseneck barnacles.

Acorn Barnacle
(Balanus glandula)

This barnacle is shaped a bit like a small volcano with a beak over the crater. They are clustered so close together that some beachgoers may think they're just jagged rocks. Each acorn barnacle has a white plate at its base that sticks to whatever the animal is glued to. You can often see patches of these white plates on the rocks where barnacles have been knocked away by predators or strong surf.

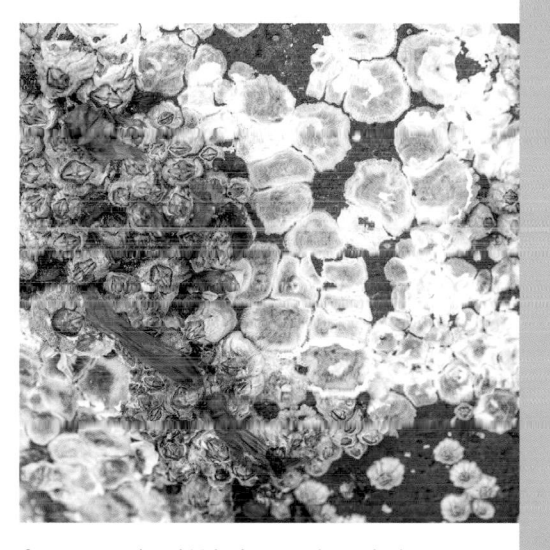

Can you see the whitish plates on this rock where the acorn barnacles have been torn loose?

APPEARANCE: Acorn barnacles grow to just under 1 inch wide and about ½ inch tall, though they're often smaller. Their cone-shaped shells are white to light gray. The shell (also called a test) is made up of overlapping plates. The inner "beak" shape is like a trapdoor made out of more plates. It can open and close to seal in water, let the barnacle feed, or protect it from predators.

Who knew? Barnacles have been around for about 330 million years! Lots of the sea creatures we see in fossils still exist in some form in the ocean today.

FOOD: Barnacles are suspension feeders: they eat the tiny animals and plants (called plankton) floating suspended in the water near them. This is one of those species that will amaze you if you slow down and look closely. It's not hard to find barnacles feeding. When a barnacle is underwater, you can often see its cirri fan out to collect food.

HABITAT: These little barnacles will attach themselves to anything hard. You can find them on rocks, boat bottoms, docks, and other animals, such as mussels, crabs, and even whales. To watch them feed, look for shallow puddles of water on large rocks in tide pools.

Look carefully at barnacles under shallow water, and you can see their feathery cirri dart in and out as they feed. They look like eyelashes!

REPRODUCTION: Barnacle eggs hatch into larvae. The larvae go through two different stages before settling down to become adults. The only job in a larva's second stage is to pick a good place to stay forever. It doesn't even eat during this stage!

RANGE: Found from Alaska down to Baja California, Mexico.

WHAT IS PLANKTON?

Plankton provides food for creatures as small as barnacles and as massive as whales. But what is it? *Plankton* is a term for all of the organisms that drift around at the mercy of the tides in the ocean. Some plankton are animals—including the larvae of many of the sea creatures discussed in this book. Those are known as zooplankton (pronounced ZO-uh-plank-ton), or "animal drifters." Many of the organisms are tiny, even microscopic, but others, such as sea jellies, are much larger.

Other plankton are more like plants, so they are called phytoplankton (pronounced FI-toe-plank-ton), which means "plant drifter." Some kinds of phytoplankton even glow in the dark! That glow is called bioluminescence. You can see the water light up blue and green as the plankton is moved by waves and fishes. Amazing!

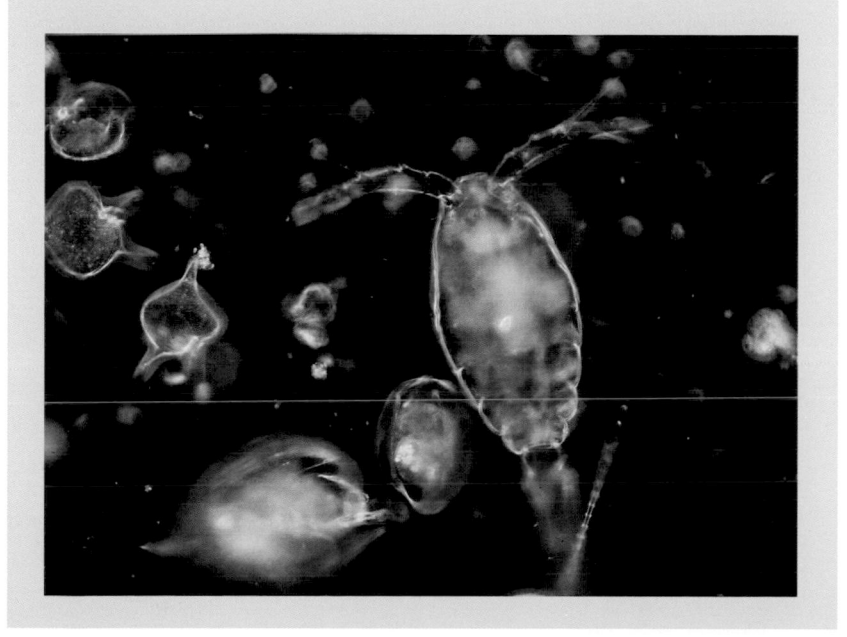

Gooseneck Barnacle
(Pollicipes polymerus)

Gooseneck barnacles look different from their smaller acorn cousins. Their plated shell sits at the end of a long stalk called a peduncle. Look carefully. Do you see a goose head and neck (or maybe a dragon)? Sometimes the origins of common animal names are easy to understand.

Who knew? Not only do these barnacles look a bit like goosenecks if you squint, there was a time when people believed they were actually goose *eggs*! Back in the Middle Ages, some people thought these barnacles were the eggs of a bird called a barnacle goose and that when the barnacles were ready, they'd fall into the water and geese would emerge. To be clear, that's not really how it works. Barnacle geese lay their eggs up in the Arctic. And barnacles stay barnacles without ever turning into birds.

APPEARANCE: Gooseneck barnacles can grow as long as 6 inches, including the shell and the stalk. The brown stalk looks kind of rubbery and is sometimes partly translucent (light can go through it). If you watch carefully, you can sometimes see the stalks move! Like other barnacles, their shells are made of overlapping plates. In this species, the plates look a bit like fingernails or scales. Those at the end can open and close to let the barnacle reach out with its feathery cirri.

FOOD: These barnacles are filter feeders that eat plankton, which they drag to their mouths with their legs. They themselves are eaten by many seabirds as well as humans. In several countries, the peduncles on goosenecks are considered delicacies.

HABITAT: Gooseneck barnacles grow on rocks and other hard places in the intertidal zone. Sometimes you can find these and acorn barnacles on shells and pieces of wood that have washed up on the wrack line. Remember that the barnacles are often still alive, so admire them with care.

REPRODUCTION: Gooseneck barnacle eggs hatch into larvae, which then transform into a second type of larvae before settling down in their adult

Check out those cirri fanning out to gather food to pull into the barnacles' mouths!

location. The second larval stage can sense how bumpy, wet, and nutrient-rich a spot is. It also senses the presence of other barnacles—they prefer a crowd.

RANGE: Common from southeast Alaska down to Baja California, Mexico.

Other Species to Look For

GIANT ACORN BARNACLE
(Balanus nubilus)
As its name suggests, this barnacle is the giant cousin of the acorn barnacle. In fact, it's one of the largest barnacles in the world at about 3 inches across and almost 5 inches high. Check out those long cirri!

PELAGIC GOOSENECK
BARNACLE *(Lepas anatifera)*
This type of gooseneck barnacle has a brighter white shell edged in orange and yellow. Can you see the difference?

THATCHED BARNACLE
(Semibalanus cariosus)
This medium-sized barnacle can be found from Alaska down to Central California. It has ridges that make it look a bit like a thatched hut.

Chiton

Chitons (pronounced KITE-uns) have been around for a really long time—over 500 million years! They are in a group called mollusks, which are related to snails and clams. Like many mollusks, chitons have soft, squishy bodies protected by a hard shell.

A chiton's shell is made up of eight separate plates that overlap like a suit of armor. The plates are held together around the edge by a fleshy

Lined chiton (Tonicella lineata) on the left, hairy chiton (Mopalia ciliata) on the right, with a thick pink crust of coralline algae coating its plates

border called a girdle. The girdle is a thickened part of the mantle, which is what scientists call the body wall. Those plates make it so chiton shells can bend as they creep across uneven surfaces. Some chitons can even roll up if they get pulled from a rock by a wave or a predator, curving their shells around their soft underparts for protection. They look a little like bigger versions of the roly-poly bugs you might see in your yard.

Chitons slowly creep along rocks using a big sticky foot hidden under their shell. If they're disturbed, that foot will clamp on so tightly that it's almost impossible to move them without breaking their shell.

Who knew? How does a chiton know a place is dark? It has hundreds of little eyelike spots on its shell that help it sense light and shadows.

girdle

head with
mouth in
center

mantle groove
with gills inside

foot

*Check out the underside of this chiton!
Remember, never try to pull an intertidal
creature from its rock.*

Never try to pry a chiton (or any tide pool animal) from its rock. Doing that could injure it.

Along the sides of the foot are the chiton's gills, which let them to take in oxygen from the water like fish do. Unlike most fish, chitons can still breathe when they're out of the water as long as their gills don't dry out.

APPEARANCE: Chitons are oval shaped, and you can usually see the eight plates of armor on their back. Different types of chitons can be as small as ½ inch or as big as 13 inches. Most are closer to 2 inches. They can be colorful or dull, shiny or rough. Their girdles may be covered in little "hairs" or not. Some girdles even have polka dots! There's a lot of variety, but if you see those eight plates surrounded by a fleshy border, you've found a chiton.

FOOD: Chitons eat the slimy stuff on rocks made up of algae and bacteria. They creep along, scraping the rock with a body part called a radula, a flexible tonguelike band that's covered with thousands of supersharp teeth. They can't bite you, though—the teeth are too small to even see without a microscope. Some other animals also have a radula: check out the limpets on page 48 and the moon snails on page 83.

HABITAT: Most chitons like dark, hidden places, so you may need to look at really low tide to find them. Check the undersides of large rocks in tide pools, as well as in small holes in boulders or cliffsides.

REPRODUCTION: Chitons hatch from eggs and start out as larvae drifting in the water. They settle down pretty quickly, though, and change into their adult form.

RANGE: All of the chitons in this book can be found from Alaska to California.

Species to Look For

BLACK KATY CHITON *(Katharina tunicate)*
Black Katy chitons have a black girdle that grows partly over the top of their shell plates. They are sometimes called leather chitons because their girdles make it look like they're wearing a leather jacket.

GUMBOOT CHITON *(Cryptochiton stelleri)*
There's always one guy who doesn't follow the rules! The gumboot chiton (also called the giant Pacific chiton) is the largest in the world, and it's found right here on the Pacific coast. It can grow up to 13 inches long! But what makes it really different is that its girdle goes all the way over the top of its plates. The plates are still there, but you can't see them at all. Instead, this chiton looks like a big bumpy reddish blob.

LINED CHITON *(Tonicella lineata)*
These are some of the prettiest chitons on the coast. Look for colorful patterns of dark and light lines on the shell plates.

MOSSY OR HAIRY CHITON *(Mopalia muscosa, Mopalia ciliata)*
Mossy and hairy chitons look similar. Both have short spiky "hairs" poking out of their girdle. The easiest way to tell the two apart is to gently touch the girdle with one wet finger. If the hairs are soft, it's a hairy chiton. If they're stiff, it's a mossy chiton.

Crab

Crabs are crustaceans, just like barnacles, and have a hard outer shell instead of bones. The large upper shell on a crab's back is called a carapace (pronounced CARE-uh-pace). Crab bodies are usually flat, and they have eyeballs on the ends of two short antennae. Their gills let them breathe underwater, but they can also breathe on land as long as their gills stay wet. If you get a chance to see crabs move, you'll notice that most can swim or walk sideways.

Purple shore crab

Crabs have ten legs, including their pincers. Male crabs often have bigger pincers than females. If you flip them over, males and females also have differences on their abdomens (undersides). Compare the male and the female in the photos below—what do you see? The female has a wide arching shape to her lower shell, which looks like a beehive. The male has kind of a tall, steeper hill on his shell, which looks like a

Male crab

Female crab

lighthouse. Different crab species have different shell patterns, but all females have a wider shape below while the males have a narrower one. At certain times of the year, you might also see clusters of eggs held on the female's abdomen. That makes telling them apart even easier!

Who knew? As a crab grows, its soft inside parts get bigger but its shell stays the same size. Because of this, crabs and other crustaceans molt (see barnacle cirri on page 22). Molting is when the crab breaks out of its shell and grows a new one. The old shell then gets left behind for beachgoers to discover. Crabs can also regrow lost legs if they are bitten off by a predator. It only takes a couple of molts for the new legs to be back to full size! Right after it molts, a crab is soft and extra vulnerable to predators. It needs time to grow and harden a new shell before it can even walk. Crabs will often hide out under the sand or in rock crevices to keep safe. Often, large groups of crabs will molt at the same time. That can cause hundreds of empty shells to wash up on the wrack line together.

There are thousands of different species of crabs around the world. What follows are some common species found on the Pacific coast shore.

Dungeness Crab
(Cancer magister)

Dungeness crabs were named after the longest natural sandbar in the United States—the Dungeness Spit, which sticks out into the Strait of Juan de Fuca from Washington State.

APPEARANCE: Crabs are measured across their back shell (carapace) just in front of the spikes at the widest point. Dungeness crabs can be up to 10 inches across but are usually closer to 7. They range in color from reddish-brown to purplish.

FOOD: Dungeness crabs eat animals such as fish, shrimp, small clams, and worms. That makes them carnivores. They also help clean up dead things on the ocean floor, which means they are scavengers too. They do important work to clean up debris in intertidal areas and underwater. These crabs are eaten by lots of larger beach predators as well as humans.

HABITAT: Dungeness crabs live both underwater and onshore. Look for them in sandy areas around tide pools and in eelgrass beds.

REPRODUCTION: Female Dungeness crabs lay between 1 and 2 *million* eggs per brood, and they usually have three or four broods in their lifetime. That's a lot of eggs! Like many other ocean and intertidal creatures, those eggs hatch into larvae that look nothing like crabs. Instead, they float around as zooplankton (see page 25), providing food for lots of other creatures. Some of the larvae survive, though, and become tiny versions of the crabs we recognize. It takes a juvenile Dungeness crab two to three years to molt enough times to be full size.

RANGE: Found from Alaska down to Southern California.

> **Who knew?** When a Dungeness crab first produces eggs, they are bright orange. The female carries them around on her abdomen until they're close to hatching and turn more blackish. Then she releases them into the water.

Purple Shore Crab
(Hemigrapsus nudus)

Look at those purple polka-dot claws! That's a key feature to look for when identifying this crab.

APPEARANCE: Purple shore crabs are much smaller than their Dungeness cousins. They only grow up to about 2½ inches across. These little crabs are mostly purple with patterns of other colors, such as green and yellow. As juveniles, the crabs' whole bodies can be a range of different colors, including green all over. You can still see those purple spots showing through on the claws, though.

FOOD: Purple shore crabs are mainly seaweed eaters. They often hide in rock cracks during the day and come out at night to feed on algae.

HABITAT: These crabs live underneath rocks in tide pools or inside cracks in larger rocks. If you walk slowly around a large rock and look carefully in the cracks, you have a good chance of spotting a purple shore crab. Another way to look for them is by gently rolling back small and medium-sized rocks. Be sure to carefully replace the rock afterward.

The female purple shore crab will carry up to 36,000 fertilized eggs in a special pouch on her belly until they are ready to hatch.

REPRODUCTION: Purple shore crabs reproduce by laying eggs. They hatch out into larvae that eventually transform into tiny crabs.

RANGE: Found from Alaska down to Baja California, Mexico.

Who knew? Sometimes other intertidal creatures will make a crab's shell their home while the crab is still using it. Creatures like barnacles (page 21) often attach themselves to a crab shell without harming the animal inside. What does the barnacle get out of that relationship? Is there any way it helps the crab? Think about movement as well as camouflage.

Other Species to Look For

NORTHERN KELP CRAB
(Pugettia producta)
This species loves to dine on kelp and other seaweed, but it also eats barnacles and mussels. The big claws tell you this kelp crab is a male. Females of this species have much smaller front claws.

PYGMY ROCK CRAB
(Glebocarcinus oregonensis)
This is also called a hairy cancer crab. Can you see why?

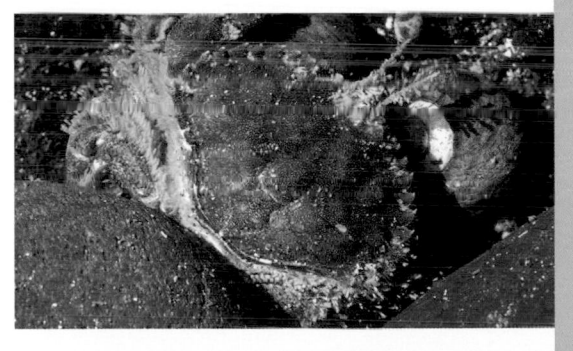

STRIPED SHORE CRAB
(Pachygrapsus crassipes)
Check out those jazzy colors! This crab looks like it stepped out of a 1980s music video.

Fish

Along with the slower or nonmoving creatures in tide pools, you might also see little fish darting around in the water or hiding under rocks. A few common tide pool fish species are described here.

Northern Clingfish
(Gobiesox maeandricus)

The clingfish's belly has its own powerful suction cup! The sucker is formed by the fused fins on the underside of the fish. It allows the fish to attach itself to rocks with amazing strength.

APPEARANCE: Even though it's secretly superstrong, the northern clingfish is flat and kind of blobby looking. It can be a range of colors, including brown, green, reddish, or gray. One way to identify this species is often by a whitish band connecting the eyes, which you can see when looking down from the top. These fish are fairly small, growing to only about 6 inches long. Most would fit easily in your hand.

Who knew? The northern clingfish is a world-champion sucker! Even on rough or slippery surfaces, the clingfish's suction disc can hold up to 230 times its own body weight. If you had a human-sized sucker that strong and you weighed 100 pounds, you could lift *23,000 pounds!*

FOOD: This predator eats a variety of small mollusks, crustaceans, and isopods. One way the clingfish uses its powerful suction disc is by pulling limpets off the rocks to eat. Limpets do not let go easily, so that strong grip really helps. The suction also keeps water around the fish's gills when it's stuck to a rock, so when the tide goes out, the clingfish can breathe until it comes in again.

HABITAT: Northern clingfish can be found under rocks in and around tide pools in the intertidal zone. Go ahead and gently tip up some rocks to search for this species, but always remember to replace the rocks carefully to keep the animals safe.

REPRODUCTION: The female clingfish lays eggs under a rock in the intertidal zone. The male stands guard until the eggs hatch. They hatch as larvae first, then transform into little fish.

RANGE: Found from Alaska down to Baja California, Mexico.

Saddleback Gunnel

(Pholis ornata)

Some people (especially in Europe) call this fish a saddled blenny. *Blenny* refers to several different types of fish, though, instead of just this one. It's an example of why researchers use scientific names instead of common names to keep species straight.

APPEARANCE: The saddleback gunnel looks a bit like an eel. It's thin, wriggly, and can grow up to 13 inches long. This gunnel ranges from green to brown and has a repeated arch-shaped pattern on its topside.

FOOD: These fish are predators that eat small crustaceans and mollusks.

HABITAT: Saddleback gunnels often live beneath rocks in the intertidal zone, similar to the clingfish. You can also find them swimming through eelgrass (see page 149).

REPRODUCTION: After eggs are laid, both males and females of this species guard them until they hatch.

RANGE: Found from British Columbia down to Southern California.

Tidepool Sculpin
(Oligocottus maculosus)

This well-camouflaged, splotchy fish's favorite pastime is resting hidden among rocks or sea anemones. If it doesn't move, it can be really hard to spot! Several different species of sculpins live along the Pacific coast, but the tidepool sculpin is the most common.

APPEARANCE: All sculpins have a large head tapering into a slimmer body and tail. The tidepool sculpin—a small species of this type of fish—can grow to around 3 inches long. If you look carefully at the fins on its sides, you can see that they are made of long spines radiating out with webbing between them. Sculpins can be a range of colors and have big dark splotches down their backs.

FOOD: This fish is a predator that eats a variety of small mollusks, crustaceans, and isopods.

HABITAT: Sculpins are common in tide pools in the intertidal zone. They're small and blend in, though, so get down low and look closely.

REPRODUCTION: Sculpins lay eggs, which hatch into a plankton stage and then, about two months later, develop into tiny fish.

RANGE: Found from the Bering Sea to Southern California.

Hermit Crab

Blueband hermit crab (Pagurus samuelis)

Even though it says "crab" in the name, hermit crabs aren't true crabs. Unlike the crabs described on page 32, hermit crabs don't grow their own hard protective shell over most of their body. They do grow shells on their front parts, including their legs and pincers. But their back end is made up of a soft curved tail that could make them easy prey. Don't worry, though! Hermit crabs have figured out a way to stay safe. They adopt the empty shells of other animals, such as sea snails, trading up to bigger and bigger "houses" as they grow. They find their new shells by smelling dead or dying snails and trying the shell on for size.

Who knew? Sometimes hermit crabs will line up by size to grab the next biggest shell after their neighbor trades up. Picture lining up by height and giving last year's winter coat to the next smaller kid in line.

There are several different species of hermit crabs along the Pacific coast, including blueband and Pacific hairy hermit crabs.

APPEARANCE: Look carefully at even the tiniest snail shells you see in a tide pool. Are there little crab legs sticking out? Congratulations—you found a hermit crab! They can be as small as a centimeter or two (less than ½ inch) or as big as a couple of inches across, including the legs. Pay special attention to those legs too. Some of them are striped with vivid colors, such as blue or green or orange.

FOOD: Like true crabs, hermits will eat pretty much anything they can find. That includes worms, plankton, and small sea creatures of all types. Unfortunately for hermit crabs, they are themselves on the menu for lots of larger sea creatures and shorebirds.

Pacific hairy hermit crab (Pagurus hirsutiusculus). It's fine to gently touch a hermit crab, but remember that their shells aren't attached to their bodies. If you pick one up, please don't grab it by the shell or it might fall out.

HABITAT: You'll find hermit crabs in tide pools in the intertidal zone. They are usually nocturnal, which means they're most active at night. They will still move around during the day, though, so keep your eyes open. Hermit crabs can be territorial, so putting one into another's turf can be dangerous for both of them.

REPRODUCTION: Female hermit crabs carry fertilized eggs with them before releasing them into the sea. Like many ocean species, they start out in a larval (plankton) stage. The larvae grow and change until they're ready to move into an empty snail shell.

RANGE: Found from Alaska to Southern California (Pacific hairy hermit) and Baja California, Mexico (blueband hermit). Other hermit crab species can also be found throughout this range.

Who knew? There are over 800 species of hermit crabs, but they can be divided into two basic types: one that lives in the water most of the time (aquatic) and one that lives on land most of the time. Coastal hermit crabs are aquatic. They can live out of water for a little while, but they will not be able to survive in one of those sandy tanks you find at a pet store. Those are for land-adapted hermit crabs. Remember: it's *never* a good idea to remove a creature from its home in the wild.

All of the hermit crabs you find on Pacific beaches are aquatic (water-dwelling).

Hydroid

Mixed hydroids

Some hydroids (pronounced HIGH-droids) look like flowers with long thin stems. Others look like feathery ferns. But just like anemones, hydroids are actually animals! They are related to sea jellies (also called jellyfish; see page 135). Hydroids can often be found living together in colonies. Sometimes they even share parts, connecting lots of individuals together. This is one of those amazing tiny animals that you are sure to miss if you don't slow down, get low, and look. They are fascinating on their own, and they are food to lots of bigger creatures that you may spot nearby.

APPEARANCE: Hydroids can live alone or in colonies. They can be too tiny to see well with the naked eye or as big as a few inches tall. See the photo descriptions for more identifying characteristics of some common—but very different looking—hydroids found around Pacific tide pools. Also check out page 107 in the Shoreline chapter to learn about a different type of hydroid called a by-the-wind sailor that lives in the open ocean but often washes up on beaches.

FOOD: Hydroids are filter feeders that eat plankton. Like sea anemones, hydroids have special stinging cells called nematocysts. In hydroids, those stingers are used for protection rather than for catching prey.

HABITAT: You can find hydroids attached to rocks in tide pools. Look down low under the water, especially in places that are protected by large rocks. Another great place to spot them is under docks and piers.

Lie on your belly on a dock and hang your head over the side (have someone hold your legs for safety!). See if you can spot any hydroids underneath.

REPRODUCTION: Hydroid reproduction is complicated even for scientists. The simple explanation is that there are several life stages for a hydroid. The species covered in this book produce medusae—tiny living structures shaped a little like bells (see more about this on page 136). Sometimes they look like teeny free-floating sea jellies; other times they look more like beads. Those medusae then produce eggs, which hatch into larvae (more zooplankton!) that will eventually settle down to start a new hydroid colony.

RANGE: Ostrich-plume hydroids live from Alaska all the way down to Central America. Solitary pink-mouth hydroids can be found from British Columbia down to Southern California. Turgid garlands can be found from Alaska to Baja California, Mexico.

Species to Look For

OSTRICH-PLUME HYDROID

(Aglaophenia struthionides)
Each little feathery branch of this hydroid holds hundreds of individual animals that all live together. Those tiny animals have microscopic stinging tentacles like a sea jelly (see page 135). Ostrich-plume hydroids can grow to 5 inches tall. They are often yellowish or tan, but they can also be light red. You  can sometimes find clusters of this type of hydroid washed up on the wrack line.

SOLITARY PINK-MOUTH HYDROID

(Ectopleura marina)

The thin stalk of the solitary pink-mouth hydroid can be up to 3 inches long. Each stalk holds a single individual. You can often find a bunch of these creatures clustered together. Can you see how this hydroid looks a bit like an upside-down sea jelly on a stem?

TURGID GARLAND HYDROID

(Symplectoscyphus turgidus; formerly *Sertularella turgida)*

This type of hydroid lives in a colony that looks like a zigzaggy yellow plant. The stalks are up to 2 inches long and are golden colored. This is another colonial creature that sometimes washes up on the wrack line.

Limpet

Limpets are a type of gastropod, which is a word that means "stomach foot." If you think about how they move, the name makes perfect sense. They have one big foot that stretches the length of their underbelly, just like their cousin the snail. They're really common, but they're easy to overlook since they are often camouflaged to blend in with their surroundings.

These ribbed limpets (also called fingered limpets) are a dark version of their kind. The color and patterns can really vary, but they all have the raised ribs that give them their common name.

APPEARANCE: Like snails, limpets have squishy bodies protected by a hard shell. While a snail shell is spiraled, a limpet shell looks more like a flattened party hat. Good news for shell hunters: this is one shell you can often find unbroken along the rocky shores of the Pacific. Different

Who knew? Limpets often have patterns that mimic their environment. Some have specially evolved to blend in with barnacles or mussels. Can you spot the limpets? This is some next-level camouflage! (Check out the key on page 215 to see if you found any we missed.)

kinds of limpets will have different textures and patterns on their shells, but they all have that same flat cone shape. How many shell varieties can you find?

FOOD: Like chitons (see page 29), limpets scrape microscopic food from rocks using their radula—a sort of tooth-covered tongue. They'll eat algae as well as tiny creatures like the larvae of barnacles and other tide pool creatures. They are eaten by clingfish, sea stars, otters, birds, and other predators.

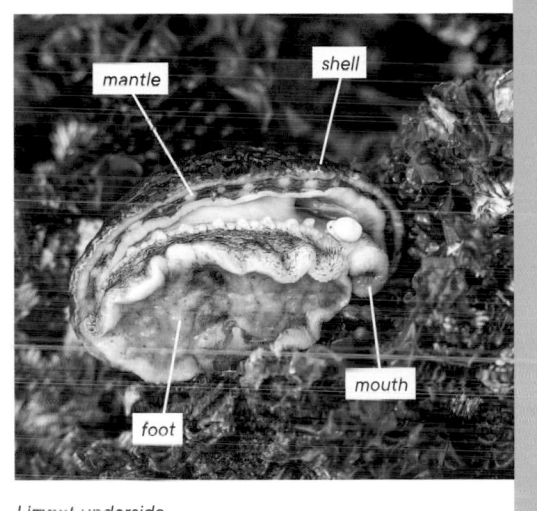

Limpet underside

Who knew? The radulas on limpets and chitons are made out of a mineral-protein mixture that is one of the strongest materials in all of the biological world. Their teeth can be up to thirteen times stronger than steel!

HABITAT: Limpets live throughout the intertidal zone. Look for them attached to large rocks, goose barnacles, mussels, and even on some types of seaweed. They will crawl around to graze and then often return to a favorite spot called a home scar that they've worn away into a shape that matches their shell.

REPRODUCTION: Limpets hatch out of eggs as larvae. After a couple of weeks, they settle down somewhere solid (such as a rock) and start building their cone-shaped shells. Limpets will add to their shells as they age and grow.

RANGE: Some form of limpet lives along every stretch of the Pacific coast. All of the limpets featured in this book have a range from Alaska down to Baja California, Mexico.

Species to Look For

ROUGH KEYHOLE LIMPET
(Diodora aspera)
See that hole at the top of the shell? That's the keyhole that gives this limpet its name.

RIBBED LIMPET *(Lottia digitalis)*
Look for the radiating ribs that give this limpet its name.

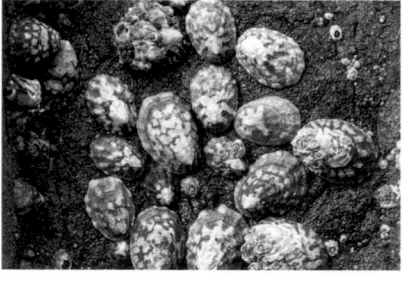

SHIELD LIMPET *(Lottia pelta)*
Can you picture this shell as the decorated shield of an ancient warrior?

Mussel

Mussels (pronounced like the ones in your body—muscles—but spelled differently) are a type of bivalve shellfish. Bivalves are soft animals that are protected by a pair of shells. *Bi-* means "two," and each half of the shell is called a valve. Other bivalves include clams and oysters.

Mussels

APPEARANCE: The shells on mussels can be either blue-black or brown on the outside. They are longish, with one pointier end and one more rounded end. The two most common types are Pacific blue mussels (*Mytilus trossulus*), which are smaller than 5 inches long when fully grown, and California mussels (*Mytilus californianus*), which can be up to almost 10 inches long. You can often find empty mussel shells along the sand; the insides can be a beautiful pearly purple and blue.

Pacific blue mussels

California mussels (with a large barnacle on the one on the right)

FOOD: Like most bivalves, mussels are filter feeders. They pump up to 20 gallons of water through their gills every day and filter out plankton to eat. They are also themselves food for lots of animals both under the water and above it—especially snails, sea stars, and gulls.

HABITAT: Large groups of mussels gather on rocks in and around tide pools. If there aren't enough predators around, mussels may be *all* you see. They can easily take over an entire ecosystem.

REPRODUCTION: A female mussel can lay up to *100,000 eggs* every single year, and mussels can live sixty to seventy years. That's a lot of mussels! They release eggs into the water, which are then fertilized and hatch into a larval stage. The larvae float around for several months before settling down to change into their adult form.

RANGE: The California mussel extends a bit farther south than the Pacific blue, but both can be found as far north as Alaska.

Who knew? Mussels produce a sticky substance from their foot that hardens into superstrong strings called byssus (pronounced BISS-us) threads, also known as the mussel's beard. Mussels use their byssus to attach themselves to rocks and other hard surfaces, as well as to other  mussels. (There's strength in numbers!) They can even be used for protection: when a predatory snail comes around, the mussel can reach out with its foot and use its sticky threads to glue the predator to a nearby rock.

Nudibranch

These amazing sea slugs are much more wildly colored and patterned than slugs on land. There are around 3,000 species of nudibranchs (pronounced NOO-di-branks) in the world's oceans. Some are smooth or covered in small bumps and have a tuft of gills on their back end. Others have wavy projections called cerata all over their backs. Cerata do two jobs for the nudibranchs that have them. First, they help them breathe—like the tuft of gills on their lumpier cousins. (The word *nudibranch* literally means "naked gills.") The second job for cerata is to defend the animal from possible predators.

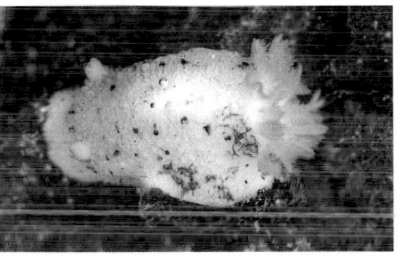

See the tuft of gills on this Monteroy dorid nudibranch?

Some people call this white-and-orange-tipped nudibranch a candy corn nudibranch. Can you see why?

Who knew? When some types of nudibranchs eat stinging creatures like anemones and hydroids, they collect and store the stinging cells (nematocysts) from those animals. The cells pass through the nudibranch's digestive system without hurting it and get stored in the tips of its cerata. Then the nudibranch can use those cells to protect itself from its own predators. It's secondhand battle armor!

Thick-Horned Nudibranch
(Hermissenda crassicornis)

A similar species (*Hermissenda opalescens*) also lives along the Pacific coast, but it doesn't have white lines on its cerata. (Do you see them?) Its common name is opalescent nudibranch. Until recently, the two were considered the same species. As scientists learn more, even the names change!

APPEARANCE: You can recognize this nudibranch by its milky-colored body and the bright orange on its cerata. They also have electric-blue lines down each side of the big tentacles on their heads that give them their common name. They can grow to around 3 inches long, but are often much smaller in tide pools.

FOOD: This animal's favorite food is hydroids. If you see any, be sure to look around for a thick-horned nudibranch. They'll also eat little anemones and other small marine organisms.

HABITAT: Look for these nudibranchs in tide pools in the intertidal zone. When you see them in the water, their cerata will be extended and wavy like a sea anemone. If you spot one up on a rock out of the water, it will be curled up, kind of like an anemone trying to hold on to its moisture until the tide comes back in.

REPRODUCTION: Nudibranchs lay eggs. You can sometimes see clusters of this one's little white sausage-shaped eggs attached to algae or eelgrass.

RANGE: Found all the way from Alaska down to Baja California, Mexico.

Rufous-Tipped Nudibranch

(Acanthodoris nanaimoensis)

This type of nudibranch is called a dorid. Can you see how it looks different from the thick-horned nudibranch?

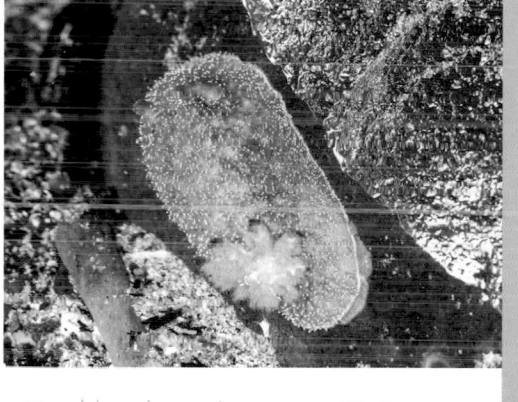

APPEARANCE: Dorids don't have spiky cerata on their backs like some other nudibranchs. Instead, this light-colored flattened oval creature has yellow-tipped short bumps all over. It also has a pair of antenna-like rhinophores (pronounced RI-no-fors) near its head end and a circle of gills near its back end. Both the rhinophores and the gills have red tips. That's where this animal gets one of its common names (rufous-tipped nudibranch). In nature, *rufous* means reddish. One of its other common names is the Nanaimo dorid, after a city in British Columbia.

FOOD: These nudibranchs eat bryozoans (see page 104) and tunicates (see page 90)—tiny creatures that live in colonies and don't move around.

HABITAT: You can find these dorids underwater on rocks. Despite their rufous tips, these creatures blend in really well with their surroundings. Get down low in tide pools, move slowly, and look carefully—especially under and around larger rocks.

REPRODUCTION: Nudibranchs lay eggs. The egg clusters can be as varied and beautiful as the creatures themselves. They often look like wavy ribbons attached in spirals to rocks and piers.

RANGE: Found from Alaska to Central California.

Who knew? This nudibranch has a fun trick. It can creep along the *underside* of the surface of the water! You can look down into a tide pool and see this creature's underparts as it wriggles across the tension on the surface.

Other Species to Look For

Frosted nudibranch (Dirona albolineata)

British Columbia aeolid (Catriona columbiana)

Monterey sea lemon (Doris montereyensis)

Sea clown nudibranch (Triopha catalinae)

Shaggy mouse nudibranch (Aeolidia papillosa)

Barnacle-eating dorid (Onchidoris bilamellata)

Sea Cucumber

The naturalists naming sea creatures must have had one weird salad bar. Many creatures are named after common land vegetables, but they're often not like their namesakes at all. Take the sea cucumber, for example. First of all, a sea cucumber is an animal, not a plant! They're a type called an echinoderm (pronounced eh-KI-nuh-derm), which literally means "spiny skinned." Other members of that group include sea stars, brittle stars, sea urchins, and sand dollars. Instead of blood, echinoderms' circulatory systems are built around seawater!

The bright orange creature in the center that looks like it's wearing a ruffled skirt is a sea cucumber.

APPEARANCE: Sea cucumbers are roughly the *shape* of a cucumber, but that's really where the similarity ends. They move by pulling themselves along the rocks and seafloor with hundreds of little tube feet tipped with suction cups. Sea cucumbers can be many colors, from deep red to bright orange to off-white.

FOOD: These animals are scavengers. They'll eat whatever small organisms their tentacles can grab from the seabed. A sea cucumber's tentacles are covered in mucus (like the snot in your nose when you have a cold). When the tentacles wave around in the water, tiny bits of floating food stick to the mucus. Then the sea cucumber sticks the tentacles in its mouth to eat the mucus and food bits. (Yum!) Sea cucumbers are themselves food for many larger creatures, such as sea stars, crabs, and otters.

HABITAT: You can find sea cucumbers in tide pools, especially at minus tides when the surf is out farther than usual. They like calmer water, so look in quiet pools under large rocks. Sometimes sea cucumbers will hide in a rock crack with just their tentacle end sticking out. Their tube feet may have bits of shells, rocks, or plant matter stuck to them.

REPRODUCTION: Sea cucumbers can reproduce in two different ways. They can release eggs out into the water, or they can form a bud on their body that breaks off and grows into a separate clone. Imagine if land animals could reproduce like that!

RANGE: The giant red and stiff-footed sea cucumbers can be found from Alaska down to Mexico. The orange sea cucumber can be found from Alaska to Central California.

Species to Look For

GIANT RED SEA CUCUMBER
(Apostichopus californicus)
These animals range from dark red to brown or even yellow. They are covered with bumps that look spiky but aren't actually sharp. This is the biggest sea cucumber along the Pacific coast. They can grow to about 1½ feet long and about 2 inches across. They have twenty tentacles on their feeding end

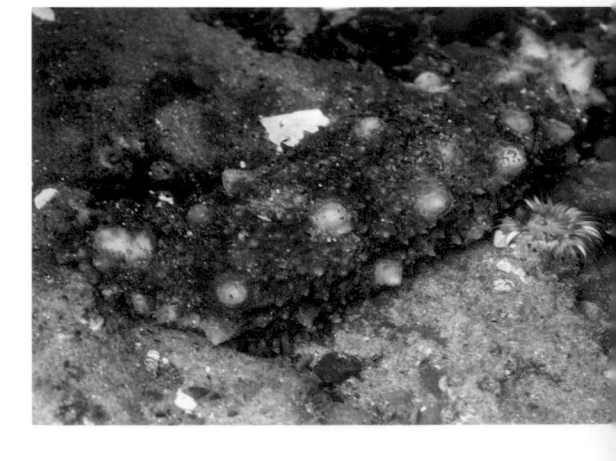

and also have lots of little tube feet on their undersides that help them creep along the ocean floor.

ORANGE SEA CUCUMBER

(Cucumaria miniata)

This creature is smaller, smoother, and brighter orange than the giant red sea cucumber. It can be up to 10 inches long, but it often hides the bulk of its body in the rocks. You are most likely to see the extended tentacles as it waits for dinner to float by. It also has lots of little tube feet that are divided into five rows going down the length of its body. Can you see the tube feet in this photo?

STIFF-FOOTED SEA CUCUMBER

(Eupentacta quinquesemita)

This sea cucumber is mostly white or cream colored. It's much smaller than its giant red and orange cousins, growing to only about 4 inches long. The tentacles on its feeding end can be pink or yellow. If you gently touch this creature, the tube feet feel kind of stiff.

Who knew? If a sea cucumber feels threatened, it poops out its internal organs to distract the predator. That would be like you being attacked by a bear and throwing him your liver while you escaped. Unlike you, the sea cucumber can grow its organs back in just a few weeks.

SEA-SIDE SALAD BAR

Not every living thing that gets its name from the salad bar is an animal. Check out this sea lettuce (*Ulva lactuca*)! It's a type of green seaweed, and it's edible. Wild animals and humans around the world often snack on it. You can find sea lettuce—which looks a bit like regular lettuce leaves—along rocky shores. Remember: never eat anything you find in the wild without a knowledgeable adult to guide you.

Another seaweed that sounds like it could be on a salad bar is sea cauliflower (*Leathesia marina*). You shouldn't eat this one, but that's OK since it looks like yellowish-brown brains. Does it look appetizing?

Sea Star

You may have heard these creatures called starfish, but they're actually not fish at all. They don't have scales or gills or a backbone like fish do. They're echinoderms like sea cucumbers. All echinoderms have something starlike about how they're constructed. Sea stars are the most obvious. As

you read about other echinoderms, see if you can spot the star in how they're built. Sometimes you may have to look from the head or tail end to spot it.

Sea stars have a circulatory system that works using mostly seawater. Water is also what powers their many tube feet. To keep the water balanced in their body, sea stars have a kind of water port on their topside that can open and close. The port, called a madreporite (pronounced MAD-ruh-pore-ite), is often a light-colored dot. In the photo here, it's actually bright orange.

There are dozens of species of sea stars along the coast. A few are featured on page 63, but keep your eye out for others.

APPEARANCE: Sea stars often have five arms, called rays, but some species can have as many as fifty! Every arm has an eye spot on the tip that lets the sea star sense light. That helps them find prey and avoid predators. Sea stars often have bumpy, spiny skin on their topside, and their underside is covered with tiny tube feet. Those little feet let the sea star move along rocks and the ocean floor.

FOOD: Sea stars eat animals such as clams, snails, mussels, crabs, and barnacles. The bigger the sea star, the bigger the prey it can eat.

Sea stars are so important to coastal environments that they're considered a keystone species. That's what scientists call an animal that is so critical to the balance of life in an area that if it goes away, the whole ecosystem can fail. Sea stars are predators that keep animals like mussels and barnacles from taking over tide pools. That allows seaweed and smaller animals like

snails, nudibranchs, and limpets to thrive. If you see a tide pool with just mussels and barnacles—and nothing else—something might have happened to the sea stars.

Who knew? Even more interesting than *what* sea stars eat is *how* they eat. Many sea stars eat larger prey by pushing part of their own stomach outside of their body! They'll grab the prey, such as a clam, and pull it open just a bit with their arms wrapped around it. Then the sea star will stick part of its stomach out through its mouth into the shell to start digesting the clam. When it's nice and soupy, the sea star will slurp its stomach and the partly digested meat back inside its body. A single meal can take them two whole days to eat!

HABITAT: Sea stars live all over the ocean, but you are most likely to find them clinging to the underside of large rocks in the intertidal zone. Be sure to look down low where the water is splashing against cliff faces or large boulders. For smaller sea stars, you may need to gently turn over medium-sized rocks. Always return rocks to their original position and watch for exposed animals. Investigating these creatures is fascinating, but *never* try to pry a sea star from a rock—that can easily harm it.

REPRODUCTION: As if the way they eat isn't cool enough, sea stars can also regrow missing limbs. Some species can even grow a whole new body from a single arm! That can be a huge help when escaping predators such as otters and seabirds. They can also reproduce by releasing eggs into the water. Those eggs hatch into—you guessed it—larvae (plankton), which drift for a few weeks before becoming tiny sea stars.

RANGE: All of the sea stars featured here live from Alaska down to California (and even farther south for some species). Ochre sea stars are most common along the Oregon coast, while the other species are common farther north.

Species to Look For

LEATHER STAR *(Dermasterias imbricata)*
This type of sea star has smoother, shorter, more webbed-looking arms than the other stars featured here. Its body has a light-colored base with a mottled pattern in reds and oranges. The leather

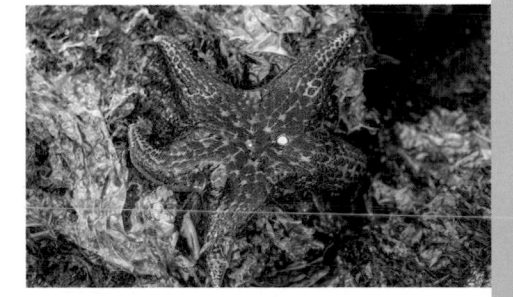

star can grow up to 12 inches from arm tip to arm tip. If you get close enough, you might also notice that it feels like wet leather and smells like garlic!

MOTTLED STAR *(Evasterias troschelii)*
This species looks a little like an ochre sea star, but it has a smaller central disc (the non-leg part of the star). It also has a very noticeable weblike pattern on its topside. They can grow to be fairly big, up to 24 inches across,

and display a wide range of colors, from brown to orange or even blue. Mottled stars are usually found north of the Puget Sound in Washington.

OCHRE SEA STAR *(Pisaster ochraceus)*
This is the most common sea star along the Pacific coast. As the name suggests, they can be ochre (a brownish orange), but they can also be purple or yellow or bright orange. These five-armed stars

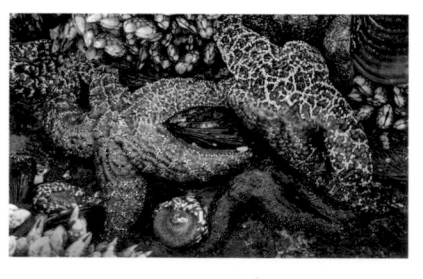

can be big: up to 20 inches from tip to tip. They love to feed on prey that can't move away, such as mussels and barnacles.

PACIFIC BLOOD STAR *(Henricia leviuscula)*
These beauties can grow to be 13 inches across, but most in tide pools are quite small. They are a deep red to reddish-orange color. That plus their smaller size makes some beachgoers want to take

them home as souvenirs. Please don't. Not only are these wild animals, but they also lose that pretty red color as they dry out. Take a photo or draw a picture instead.

Since 2013, there has been a massive drop in sea star populations on the West Coast. Millions have died because of something called sea star wasting syndrome. In some species, the disease nearly wiped out their whole population. When infected, white sores form

on the sea stars' arms, and parts of their body just kind of dissolve. The disease isn't harmful to humans, but it's hurting sea star populations, which are important for healthy beach ecosystems.

To help, scientists have tried treating sea stars with different chemicals and medicines. They've also asked tide poolers to give the stars a little extra room until their numbers recover. As you think about *gently* touching these creatures, look carefully for any that appear unwell and avoid them.

The good news is that in many places the sea star populations are bouncing back. You have a good chance of spotting them at low tide.

Sea Urchin

Like other echinoderms, the sea urchin has spiny skin, which is why they are sometimes called hedgehogs of the sea. In this case, the spines are really long and sharp. This thing has some defenses! (It's one of the reasons tide pool explorers shouldn't go barefoot.)

Note: Some sea urchins around the world have venom in their spines. Our local intertidal species aren't technically venomous, but they do carry toxins that can cause pain and infection if you get stabbed. The only way these creatures can stab you, though, is if you press too hard on their spines. Don't do that and you'll be fine. If you do acciden-

Sea urchin underside

tally get a spine in your skin, remove it and soak the area in hot water.

APPEARANCE: The sea urchin's spines surround a hard shell called a test, which is shaped sort of like a flattened ball. In addition to the spines, it has two other types of pokey parts: tube feet and tiny pincers. The tube feet aren't just on the bottom—they go almost all the way around the urchin's body. If something edible falls on its back, the sea urchin can hand the snack down to its mouth foot by foot. The mouth is underneath its body in the very center, while the anus (where poop comes out) is on its topside. Urchins also use their tube feet to *breathe*—even more than they use their gills! After urchins die, their spines and tube feet decompose, and their beautiful pale tests become visible.

FOOD: Pacific sea urchins are mostly herbivores that eat different forms of seaweed. Some, though—especially green urchins—will eat pretty much anything that floats their way. Sea urchins have a mouth organ on the underside of their body that's called an Aristotle's lantern. It's made up of strong muscles and five teeth in the shape of a star. When urchins take a bite of kelp, they can leave star-shaped bite marks.

Sea urchins are prey to otters, large sea stars, and even humans. If predators don't keep sea urchin populations in check, the urchins can wipe out entire seaweed ecosystems by eating too much.

HABITAT: Sea urchins live in both the intertidal zone (where tide pools are) and the subtidal zone, which is the underwater area near

This is a sea urchin test, which is kind of like its skeleton after it dies.

Check out this sea urchin's star-shaped mouth! It's called an Aristotle's lantern.

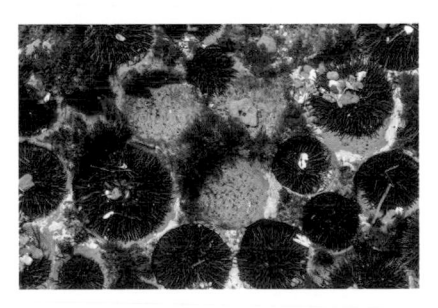
Can you see how these sea urchins have dug out burrows that perfectly fit their bodies?

the shore. In tide pools, sea urchins dig burrows out of the rocks using their teeth and spines. Over time, the burrows get deeper. Depending on their location and the species, sea urchins can live anywhere from twenty to two hundred years! Over a long enough time, some urchins dig themselves into their burrows so well that they can't leave! They just have to stay home and wait for food to float by.

Who knew? Some urchins wear shells and rocks as hats! People with home aquariums have even tried giving them little plastic hats, and they'll wear those too. Scientists think urchins may do this for added protection or to keep from drying out when the tide goes out.

REPRODUCTION: Sea urchins release eggs (lots and lots of eggs) into the water. When they're fertilized, they eventually hatch into little spaceship-shaped larvae. A larva floats around in the current eating phytoplankton (algae) until it senses that it's back near the shore in a good resting place. Meanwhile, the adult urchin is growing inside it with its spines facing inward. When it finds the right spot and is ready to transform into an adult, the larva reaches out with its tube feet and basically *turns itself inside out*!

RANGE: Purple and giant red sea urchins can be found from Alaska down to Baja California, Mexico. Green sea urchins can be found from the Arctic down to Washington.

Species to Look For

GIANT RED SEA URCHIN

(Mesocentrotus franciscanus)
This is the largest and spikiest of
our local urchins. They are often red,
but they can also be bright purple.
You can tell them from their smaller
purple cousins by their overall size
and the length of their spines. Giant

red sea urchins can grow as big as 5 inches across, and their spines are
up to two-thirds the length of their test.

GREEN SEA URCHIN *(Strongylocentrotus droebachiensis)*

This urchin has a purple test (inner
shell) and light green spines. It grows
to just over 3 inches across, and the
short spines are between one-fifth
and one-third as long as the test.
This species looks like it has brown-

ish stripes shooting out from its center. Those stripes are bands of dark
tube feet going up the sides of the test.

PURPLE SEA URCHIN

(Strongylocentrotus purpuratus)
This urchin is purple all over and a
little larger than its green cousin but
smaller than a giant red sea urchin.
It can grow to be about 4 inches
across, and the spines are between
one-quarter and one-third as long as
the test.

Seaweed

Seaweed is what we call most of the plantlike algae that live in the ocean. It comes in lots of different shapes, sizes, and colors. Scientists group seaweed by its colors into shades of green, red, or brown.

Instead of roots, seaweed often has something called a holdfast. A holdfast is just what it sounds like—a part of the seaweed that holds it fast to rocks or the ocean floor. It looks a little like a ball of roots, but it doesn't do what roots do, which is bring water and nutrients up from the soil. Holdfasts just hold on.

So, what are algae–plants or animals? Actually, the answer is *neither*! Algae don't fit perfectly into either category. They live in water and don't have true roots or leaves like most land plants, yet they can make their own

Seaweed holdfast

food from sunlight. But in other ways, they're very different from plants. Some algae, even some larger seaweeds, are made up of one single cell! Others are made up of lots of cells like land plants and animals. For comparison, a medium apple has around 50 million cells.

One last thing to know about seaweed is how important it is to the human food supply. Different seaweeds are collected or farmed for food all over the world. We also use chemicals from seaweed to make other foods better, creamier, or more stable. Have you ever heard of carrageenan? (Check your chocolate milk, ice cream, and deli meat ingredients.) That comes from seaweed!

In this book, we'll think about seaweeds (algae) as the plants of the sea since that's the role they play in their environment. But keep in mind that scientists are learning more about these amazing organisms all the time. A few common tide pool seaweeds are described on pages 71 through 77. You'll see even more types of seaweed in the Shoreline chapter on page 101.

Coralline Algae

Like the name implies, this seaweed can look a lot like coral. When coralline algae (pronounced COR-uh-line AL-jee) were first discovered way back in the 1700s, scientists thought they were animals like true coral. It was only later that scientists discovered that they were a type of red algae. There are over 1,600 species of coralline algae worldwide. See individual photos for a few examples found on the Pacific coast.

APPEARANCE: These algae can be either flat and crusty—as if someone splashed paint on a rock—or have branches and stalks like a land plant (or a coral reef). Often, those branches look like they're made of beads strung together on a wire. They are pink to light purple in color.

Who knew? When you go deep underwater, everything has a bluish cast. That's because blue light penetrates deeper in the water than other colors of light. Red algae have a pigment that reflects red light (making them look reddish) and *absorbs* blue light. That means they can absorb light energy deeper in the water than other colors of seaweed.

FOOD: Like plants on land, all types of seaweed use photosynthesis to make sugar and oxygen using sunlight and carbon dioxide from the water around them. Some fish, sea urchins, limpets, and chitons eat coralline algae. It's full of calcium like our bones and teeth, though, so it can be really hard to chew.

HABITAT: Different forms of this algae can be found all over the intertidal zone. There may be pink splotches on rocks in tide pools. You may even find branch-like coralline algae growing on mussels and other hard-shelled creatures.

Encrusting coralline algae (one of many different species that are hard to tell apart without a microscope) and articulated coralline algae (Calliarthron cheilosporioides)

REPRODUCTION: These algae reproduce using spores. Spores are a little like seeds that don't need to be fertilized. They contain all of the information needed to create a new organism.

RANGE: Various forms of coralline algae are found from Alaska down to Mexico.

Dead Man's Fingers

(Codium fragile)

Is it seaweed or something reaching up from the deep? Early explorers seemed to think it looked like fingers, which is where this seaweed got its creepy common name. This is one of the amazing single-celled seaweeds!

APPEARANCE: This seaweed has velvety dark green branches that can look like swollen dead fingers hanging from rocks at low tide. Another common name for this seaweed is sea staghorn since it looks a bit like deer antlers. Its branches can grow up to 16 inches long.

FOOD: This seaweed makes its own food from sunlight through photosynthesis. The main creatures that nibble on this type of seaweed are sea slugs, snails, sea urchins, and humans. Be careful to only eat wild coastal foods collected by experts. Sometimes there are toxic algae

blooms that can make ocean foods unsafe to eat (see more about this on page 113).

HABITAT: Common in the intertidal zone, this seaweed clings to rocks and even some shellfish. You can also find it washed up along the wrack line.

REPRODUCTION: This type of algae can reproduce through fertilization like many land plants. It can also grow a whole new seaweed from a piece of an existing one.

RANGE: Found from Alaska down to Baja California, Mexico.

Who knew? Dead man's fingers is one of the most invasive forms of seaweed. It has been carried around the world attached to ships, fishing nets, and even the shells of clams and oysters. In well-balanced ecosystems with the right number of predators, prey, and other seaweeds, this invader isn't a big problem. But if something in the ecosystem is off-balance, these algae can take over an entire area.

Rockweed

(Fucus distichus)

APPEARANCE: Rockweed is a type of brown seaweed, even though the tips can be yellow-ish green.

FOOD: Like all seaweed, rockweed gets its energy from the sun through photosynthesis. Most ocean-grazing creatures can't digest rockweed, which allows it to spread thickly if there are no other organisms already using a space. The animals that do eat rockweed include periwinkles, limpets, some isopods, and even humans.

HABITAT: As the name suggests, you can find this seaweed attached to rocks throughout the intertidal zone. Pieces of it are also often washed up along the wrack line.

REPRODUCTION: The reproduction cells are contained in the swollen yellow-green tips of this seaweed. They get released into the water, and new algae are created.

RANGE: Found from Alaska down to Central California.

Spongy Cushion

(Codium setchellii)

Believe it or not, this blackish-green blob is related to dead man's fingers (see page 73). They are different forms of a green seaweed called *Codium*. Spongy cushion doesn't look like fingers or even seaweed, though.

APPEARANCE: This bloblike seaweed can be up to 10 inches across and ranges from dark green to almost black. It feels solid to the touch when it's young and gets squishier as it ages.

FOOD: Even though this form of *Codium* can look almost black, it's still a form of green seaweed. That means it makes its own food from sunlight. Fewer creatures enjoy eating this form of *Codium*. (Can you blame them?) It is eaten by some nudibranchs (sea slugs; see page 53), so you should keep an eye out for those cool creatures when you spot a spongy cushion.

HABITAT: Spongy cushion grows on rocks in tide pools. You can find it in the intertidal zone as well as in the shallow water just offshore.

REPRODUCTION: This type of algae can reproduce through fertilization like many land plants. It can also grow from a broken-off piece of an existing spongy cushion.

RANGE: Found from Alaska down to Mexico, though it's less common south of Oregon.

Other Species to Look For

IRIDESCENT SEAWEED (*Mazzaella splendens*)
This red seaweed shines with sparkles of blue and purple when the light hits the wet blades just right. That's what the *iridescent* in its name means. If you've ever seen a slick of oil on top of a puddle and noticed how it almost looked like a rainbow, it's a lot like that.

SEA SACS (*Halosaccion glandiforme*)
This species is grouped with the red seaweeds even though its color can range from yellowish to almost purple. The more sunlight it gets, the more yellow-green it is. The pickle-shaped hollow sacs are filled with seawater and pockets of air.

Seagrass laver (Smithora naiadum). The red seaweed in this photo grows on blades of sea grass instead of the ocean floor. Each delicate frond is only one cell thick!

Snail

Most people think they know what snails are. They're like slugs with a spiral shell on their back, right? But have you ever really checked out *marine* (saltwater) snails? Some are predators that eat other tide pool and beach creatures such as barnacles, mussels, and clams. Others are herbivores that spend their days grazing on algae among the rocks. Most have gills like a fish and can breathe underwater, but they can also crawl in the open air as long as they don't dry out too much. Pacific marine snails range from smaller than your fingernail to bigger than your whole hand. Snails provide food for intertidal hunters as well as homes for hermit crabs (see page 42).

Look at the difference in size between these striped dogwinkles and the tiny periwinkles grazing near them!

See that reddish-orange seal inside the shell? That's the snail's operculum!

Inside their hard, coiled shells, snails have a soft body. As gastropods (meaning "stomach foot"), they're related to limpets (see page 48). If you pick up a snail, it will probably pull its body up inside the shell and seal the opening with a hard, fleshy door called an operculum (pronounced oh-PER-cue-lum). The shell is part of the snail's body. Unlike a lot of other creatures along the waterline, snails don't shed their shells as they grow. The shell grows along with the snail. When you (or a hermit crab) find an empty snail shell, it means that the snail that built it has died.

Black Turban
(Tegula funebralis)

As scientists learn more about the natural world, they change how they group animals. In some cases that goes as far as altering the scientific name. This snail used to be named *Chlorostoma funebralis*, but researchers learned it's part of a family of marine snails called Tegulidae. Science is not a "learn it once" way of looking at the world. As we know more, our understanding grows and changes.

APPEARANCE: Like its common name suggests, the shell of this snail is turban shaped. It can grow to just over an inch across and is about as tall as it is wide. Even though parts of its shell can be blackish purple, the *black* in the name actually refers to the color of the head and foot

of the snail hiding inside. Over time, the dark color on the outside of the turban shell wears away, revealing white underneath. The shells can also be pinkish because they're often covered in coralline algae. (See page 71 to learn more.)

FOOD: These snails are grazers (herbivores). Think of them as the cows of sea snails. They scrape algae from hard surfaces like rocks using their sharp tonguelike radula.

HABITAT: Look for black turban snails gathered in groups in the cooler shaded undersides of large rocks in and around tide pools.

REPRODUCTION: These snails hatch from eggs into larvae and then develop into tiny versions of their adult form. Black turban snails can live to be thirty years old.

RANGE: Found from Vancouver Island, BC, all the way down to Baja California, Mexico.

Black turban snail

Dogwinkle

(Nucella)

This snail has one of the most fun common names to say of all the animals in the intertidal zone. Some people also call them whelks, but why would you when you can say "dogwinkle"?

APPEARANCE: The Pacific coast is home to several different types of dogwinkles, including frilled (*Nucella lamellosa*), lined (*Nucella analoga*), and striped (*Nucella ostrina*), among others. Frilled dogwinkles can be around 3 inches long, but the others tend to only be about half that big. Even within a single species, the shells can look very different. They can be a whole range of colors—everything from pale off-white to bright oranges and purples. The shells can be striped or solid, ridged or smooth.

Dogwinkles and a whole lot of eggs, which are sometimes called sea oats

FOOD: Dogwinkles are predators. If black turban snails (see pages 79–80) are the cows of the tide pool, dogwinkles are the wolves. They can often be found feeding on barnacles and mussels.

HABITAT: Look for dogwinkles on rocks in or near tide pools, both under the water and out in the open air.

REPRODUCTION: A female dogwinkle can lay up to 1,000 eggs per year. The yellow egg capsules are laid in clusters of hundreds at a time. You can find patches of them near the snails during the winter, which is their breeding season.

Dogwinkle egg pouches—see the eggs inside?

Some people call these sea oats because they look like grains. Each tiny yellow oat grain isn't actually an egg, though. It's a *pouch* filled with tiny little snail eggs.

RANGE: All of the dogwinkles covered here can be found from Alaska down to California.

Lewis's Moon Snail
(Nevertina lewisii)

Picture a normal snail in your mind. Now imagine that snail growing until it's bigger than both of your hands. That's a moon snail!

Lewis's Moon Snail

APPEARANCE: The shell of a moon snail can be 5½ inches across, and this snail has a trick that can make it look even more massive. Like other snails, it has one large foot across its underside. The moon snail can actually inflate its foot with water until it almost covers the shell!

FOOD: Believe it or not, the squishy moon snail is a predator. It uses its sharp radula to scrape a nearly perfect circular hole in clam shells, a process that can take up to four days. The snail then adds acid and enzymes to the hole to liquefy the clam. Then it's clam soup time!

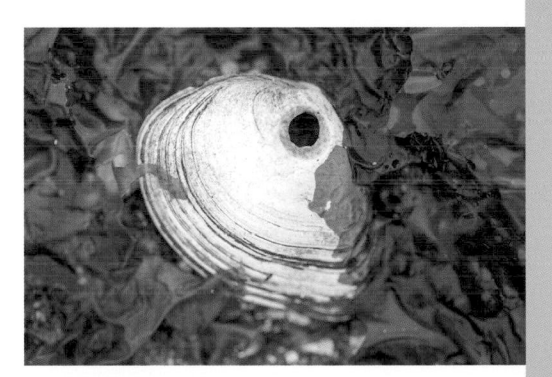

See the round hole in the clam? That's how you can tell a moon snail has been hunting here.

HABITAT: Lewis's moon snails live in the low intertidal zone (closer to the water) in sand and mud. It's easiest to find these big guys during minus tides, after a rainstorm, or at night.

REPRODUCTION: Lewis's moon snails have one of the most unusual egg sacs around. The female builds a sort of collar around herself made of mucus and sand and eggs. She then moves away, leaving the collar on the sand while the eggs develop into larvae. It's not trash, even though it may look like a broken toilet plunger!

RANGE: Found from Alaska down to Baja California, Mexico.

Moon snail egg collar

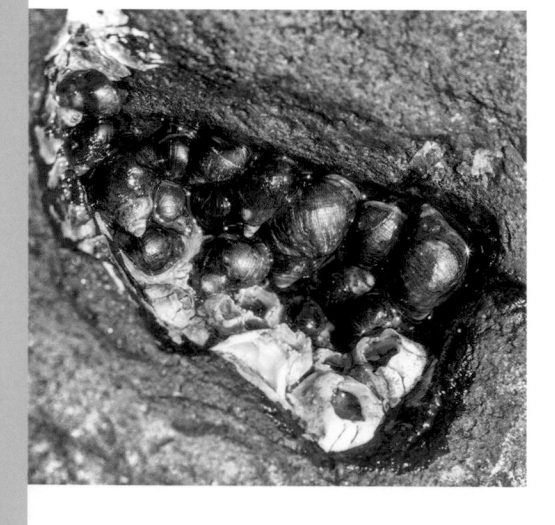

Periwinkle
(Littorina)

Have you spotted teeny snails clustered on a rock? Chances are you've found periwinkles!

APPEARANCE: Periwinkles are very small. They usually only grow to about ½ inch across. They may have patterns on their shells ranging from stripes of different colors to a checkerboard. Each shell has four whorls (spirals) on it and is purple on the inside. Individual species of periwinkles can be difficult for even experts to tell apart. Two common types are *Littorina plena* and *Littorina scutulata*.

FOOD: These little herbivores graze on algae, scraping the rocks with their radula.

HABITAT: This marine snail spends more time than most tide pool creatures out of the water. Look for them in the upper intertidal zone on rocks or piers, where they'll get splashed by the waves. A periwinkle's operculum (trapdoor) closes tightly when it's exposed to the dry air. That keeps moisture locked inside so the gills work and the little snail can breathe.

REPRODUCTION: These snails deposit eggs underwater in a sort of slimy coil. They hatch out as larvae before becoming snails.

RANGE: Found from Alaska down to Baja California, Mexico.

Purple Olive
(Callianax biplicata)

The rocky shores of the Pacific Northwest and parts of California can make it rare for beachcombers to find unbroken shells. The purple olive shell is different, though. It is so strong and streamlined that you can often find whole shells washed up in the wrack line.

Who knew? Native people used to string these pretty shells together to wear as necklaces and sometimes even used them as money. You can occasionally still find olive snail shell jewelry in coastal gift shops.

APPEARANCE: While a few species of olive snails can be found on Pacific beaches, one of the prettiest is the purple olive. Its glossy shell is blue-gray, purple, tan, and pink. The shell is kind of football shaped—long and narrow. This snail can grow to just under 1½ inches long but is usually smaller.

FOOD: Olive snails are carnivorous scavengers. That means they help clear the beach of dead creatures. Imagine what the beach would smell like if there were no scavengers! These snails are a favorite snack of moon snails as well as a variety of other beach predators.

HABITAT: If you look carefully, you can see olive snails burrowing just under the surface of the sand on the beach. They're actually pretty fast diggers for snails. You're most likely to find them on sandy beaches near the waterline.

REPRODUCTION: This snail lays tiny (about ½ mm) egg capsules that it glues to small rocks and shells. The eggs hatch out into larvae, which then become baby snails.

RANGE: Found from Alaska down to Baja California, Mexico.

Another species you might see is this sand-toned Baetic olive snail (Callianax baetica).

Sponge, Purple Encrusting

(Haliclona cinerea)

Even though it looks a bit like coralline algae (see page 71), this beautiful pinkish-purple bumpy patch is a type of animal. One that has been on Earth a long time—over 600 million years!

APPEARANCE: This species is easy to spot because of its bright color and little volcano-like bumps. A patch of purple encrusting sponge can be many inches across, but each of the volcano bumps is less than ¼ inch wide.

You know the sponges used for cleaning? Those are often made of plastic these days. But for thousands of years, people used the dried-out internal structures of actual sea sponges! In fact, many still use those natural sponges today. This particular species is too flat to use like that. But thinking about those other sponge relatives can help us understand how this creature lives. Consider how a cleaning sponge works: It soaks up water through tiny pores, and you can squeeze the water out again. Sometimes dirt goes in with the water and stays behind in the sponge. That's very similar to how this creature functions. It has no heart, no brain, no blood, not even a stomach—just lots of tiny holes for the sponge to filter water.

FOOD: Sponges are filter feeders. When water is sucked into tiny intake holes all over the sponge, floating bits of plankton and bacteria are filtered out and absorbed. Then the filtered water is released back out of the larger holes in the center of the bumps. These sponges are eaten by several types of nudibranchs (see page 53).

HABITAT: Colonies of purple encrusting sponges cover the sides of intertidal rocks and cave walls. Look for them in tide pools and exposed cracks in sea stacks and large rocks during low tide.

See the purple shore crab tucked in a crevice near the purple encrusting sponge? Those whitish blobs are short plumose anemones that are all closed up out of the water.

REPRODUCTION: Sponges can reproduce two ways: with eggs or through cloning or budding. That's when a piece splits off and grows into a new colony or it sprouts a little version of itself to form an identical new animal.

RANGE: Found from Alaska down to Southern California.

The Pacific is home to red, yellow, orange, green, and blue sponges too. They add amazing colors and textures to tide pools and sea caves.

When you find sponges, go ahead and gently touch with one wet finger. That can give you more information to tell which of the many species of sponges you've found. This red sponge could be any of several species.

Remember the limpets hiding among the barnacles on page 48? Sponges have their own hidden housemates. The creature in this photo is a red sponge nudibranch (*Rostanga pulchra*), a type of dorid (see page 55). It feeds and lives on red sponges. These nudibranchs are only about ½ inch long, and their color blends perfectly with their surroundings. So when you see a red sponge, look extra close! Can you see this dorid's tiny rhinophores down near the left end and gill circle toward the right? It's amazing how much hides in plain sight!

Tunicate

Tunicates (pronounced TOO-
ni-kits) look like colored blobs,
but they are distantly related
to complex animals with
backbones, including humans.
When they start out life as
larvae, tunicates have a wiggly
tail and a simple nervous system a lot like our spinal cord.
When they grow into adults,
the tunicate absorbs its tail and nerve cord and lives life as a much
simpler blob.

There are lots of different species of tunicates out there. Many
are complicated even for experts to tell apart. Some beachgoers also
confuse them with sponges. The best way for you to tell if it's a tunicate
is to gently touch the surface. If it feels firm and kind of rubbery, that's a
tunicate. A sponge would feel a lot squishier.

These creatures have a protective outer cover called a tunic, which
is where the *tunicate* comes from in their common name. Some types of
tunicate colonies all share one tunic. Imagine gathering with your entire
neighborhood in one giant shirt with hundreds of neck holes.

Who knew? Some
people call tunicates sea
squirts because often when
you touch this creature, it
may squirt you!

APPEARANCE: Compound tunicates can spread across the surface of a rock, sometimes looking like dripping cake batter. One drippy species is called sea vomit because of what it resembles. (Ew!) They can be a wide range of solid or translucent (kind of see-through) colors. Each of the individual creatures (called zooids) living in the colony has an intake opening to let it suck in water to filter for food. All members of a compound form like this share a group output system—kind of like a community toilet.

FOOD: All tunicates eat plankton and small debris floating in the water. Water is pulled in through one opening, and all the edible bits are filtered and consumed before the water is squirted back out through another opening.

HABITAT: Colonial tunicates live in clusters on rocks and cave walls in the low intertidal zone. Chunks of these colonies that have been torn from rocks can sometimes be found along the wrack line on the beach and are called sea pork. Go ahead and pick them up and look closely at how the zooids group together.

REPRODUCTION: Tunicates reproduce in two ways. First, larvae can hatch from eggs and eventually settle as adults. The second way is by budding, where they sprout a little version of themselves that breaks off and forms into a new identical individual.

RANGE: Found from Alaska down to Southern California.

Who knew? Several forms of tunicate are invasive. That means colonies came from somewhere else and can cause problems for local wildlife. An invasive species may take over space and resources that native plants and animals need to live. Tunicates can form colonies on boats, which then carry them around the world. Scientists are research-

ing ways to keep nonnative tunicates from entering other waters as well as ways to safely get rid of them when they do.

Worm

You may think that if you've seen one worm you've seen them all. But have you ever seen a *marine* worm? They're some of the coolest and most diverse creatures in the ocean! Sure, they can be brown like earthworms. But they can also be bright blue or orange or even striped. They can live out on the rocks, buried in the sand, or even happily hidden in a hard tube they've built out of mucus (worm snot) and sand.

Mussel Worm
(Nereis vexillosa)

APPEARANCE: Mussel worms (also called pile worms and clam worms) are a type of polychaete or bristle worm. They are iridescent greenish-blue and can be 6 to 12 inches long. The worm's body is made up of lots of segments. Each segment has a part that sticks out on either side that looks a bit like a hairy paddlefoot. Those "feet" are called parapodia (pronounced pair-uh-

PO-dee-uh). Lots of marine worms have them, and they can be used for swimming, walking, and digging.

FOOD: Mussel worms are omnivores that eat small creatures (like other worms) and algae.

HABITAT: These worms live in the intertidal zone around mussels and barnacles. You might also see one wound up in a seaweed holdfast along the wrack line on sandy beaches. Looking for cool worms is a great reason to stop and carefully poke through the washed-ashore collections. *Caution:* These worms are cool to see, but they can bite. It's best to look at this creature with your eyes only.

Check out this rubbery blob. Believe it or not, this is a mass of mussel worm eggs!

REPRODUCTION: Mussel worms reproduce by releasing eggs into the water.

RANGE: Found from Alaska down to Southern California.

Northern Feather Duster Worm
(Eudistylia vancouveri)

APPEARANCE: The feather duster builds a strong tube house out of mucus and sand that can be up to 2 feet long. It lives clustered with others of its kind in a sort of spiky ball attached to something hard like a rock or a pier. This worm has feathery plumes at one end that

Feather duster worms reminded early naturalists of old-fashioned feather dusters that people used to clean their houses. Can you see it?

poke out of the tube to collect food and oxygen. The plumes have colored bands of blue-green and deep red.

When out in the open air or threatened at all, the worm will quickly pull its plume inside its protective tube. Feather dusters have eye spots that let them sense dark and light. If you want to see the plume extended, don't let your shadow fall over it. If you gently touch the feathered end of this amazing creature, you can watch the plume disappear inside.

Who knew? Feather duster worm tubes are superstrong and difficult for the worm to build. They are made to withstand pounding waves. It's easier for feather dusters to regrow part of their body than to rebuild their home. These worm clusters can be several feet across!

FOOD: Feather duster worms are filter feeders that eat plankton and other floating bits.

HABITAT: Look for large clusters of these worm tubes attached to boulders, caves, rock crevices, and piers. They can only eat when the water brings them drifting food, so look for them in intertidal spots that are often underwater.

REPRODUCTION: These worms reproduce with eggs that hatch into larvae and then transform into worms.

RANGE: Found from Alaska down to Central California.

Orange Ribbon Worm

(Tubulanus polymorphus)

APPEARANCE: The fact that this thin, round worm is traffic-cone orange or bright red makes it noticeable enough. But a big one can also grow up to 10 feet long when fully stretched. (Although they're usually closer to 2½ feet.) When you spot one, it just keeps going and going!

FOOD: Orange ribbon worms are predators that eat other worms and crustaceans.

HABITAT: Look for these worms where you see mussels, especially in rocky or gravelly tide pools. Sometimes you might need to carefully lift a rock to spot this animal. Be sure to replace it when you're finished.

REPRODUCTION: Orange ribbons hatch from eggs, and the larvae transform into worms.

> **Who knew?** The orange ribbon worm has a body part called a proboscis (pro-BOSS-kiss). A proboscis is another word for a nose, especially a long one on something like an elephant. In the case of worms, the proboscis is more of a sucking mouthlike organ. When this worm hunts, its proboscis turns inside out, wraps around the prey, and coats it in mucus and digestive juices. When it's nice and soft, the worm slurps it down!

RANGE: Found from Alaska down to California.

Sometimes you won't see a worm, but you'll find a cool sign that worms have been there. The cellophane tube worm makes a tube a little like the feather duster's, but it's shorter, thinner, and buried just below the sand. Waves can sometimes wash the tubes to the surface—look for them along the wrack line on sandy beaches.

Cellophane worm tube

Another worm sign to look for is a squiggly pile of sand along the waterline (and sometimes just below the water). It was made by a creature called a Pacific lugworm. The lugworm swallows sand as it digs its burrow and feeds on tiny organisms. Then it poops out the sand it can't digest into a worm-shaped pile. Naturalists call those piles worm castings.

Pacific lugworm casting

Sometimes you can see crusty coiled tunnels on the side of rocks left there by calcareous tube worms.

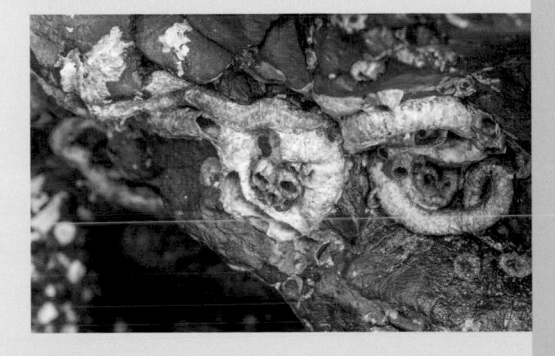

Calcareous tube worm tubes

What Do You See?

Look closely at this photo. What tide pool life forms can you see? Check for different colors and textures. Be sure to look carefully between the bright, showy bits to see what may be hiding. Turn to page 215 to see some of what the photographer spotted.

Shoreline

The sand and rocky shores host whole ecosystems and other fascinating finds. You might see big marine mammals, such as seals and sea lions. Or you may find evidence of creatures that live hidden in the deep—sea jellies or the egg sacs from deepwater squid. As you walk along the sand, be sure to check out the wrack line. It's an amazing place to find some of the coolest treasures on the beach.

Driftwood is wood that's tumbled and smoothed by ocean waves and then washed up onshore. It ranges from small pieces you can fit in your collection bucket to giant logs ready to be climbed  and explored. Be careful around those logs, though! Remember that they got to the beach by floating. Logs are not safe places to be when a big wave comes in. Even giant logs can be lifted and rolled over by less water than you'd think.

Beach Hopper

This is one of the animals that can get confusing when you use the common name since lots of beachgoers also call these sand fleas. In some parts of the world, creatures called sand fleas can have a painful bite. Down in California there is an insect called a California beach flea that is related to the fleas you might see on a dog. The beach hoppers described here aren't fleas, though. They're little amphipods (pronounced AM-fi-pods), which are a type of crustacean. They are important beach cleanup crews that never bite humans.

California Beach Hopper
(Megalorchestia californiana)

APPEARANCE: This amphipod looks like a tiny shrimp. Larger and less common than its pale cousin (see the next page), this little hopper can be up to 1½ inches long. It is tan colored and has red or orange antennae that are even longer than its body.

FOOD: California beach hoppers eat dead plants, seaweed, and creatures that collect on the sand along the wrack line.

HABITAT: These hoppers tend to hang out in burrows they dig in the dry sand at the top of the beach during the day. At night, they move down to the wrack line to dine under the cover of darkness.

REPRODUCTION: The female carries fertilized eggs in her marsupium, a special pouch under her abdomen where the offspring develop until they're ready to come out looking like tiny adults.

RANGE: Found from Vancouver Island, British Columbia, to Southern California.

Pale Beach Hopper
(Megalorchestia columbiana)

These are the little insect-like things that sometimes bounce onto your legs as you're walking down the beach. Though they're often called sand fleas, they're not fleas at all—they're not even insects! And remember, they don't bite. They're just out doing beach cleanup. Carry on, little hoppers!

APPEARANCE: Pale beach hoppers are small, topping out around ¾ inch. They're light gray or tan to blend in with the sand and can have dark marks along their backs. Their long antennae are the same color as their pale bodies.

FOOD: Beach hoppers eat algae, eelgrass, and dead animals that wash up along the wrack line. If you find a decomposing creature such a sea jelly or a crab, take a careful look and you will likely see this miniature cleanup crew. Beach hoppers are often eaten by seabirds, such as gulls.

HABITAT: These amphipods dig burrows about 12 inches into sandy beaches. They are most active at night.

REPRODUCTION: Females carry fertilized eggs in pouches on their legs until they're ready to hatch.

RANGE: Found from Alaska to Central California.

Bryozoan

Surprise: this thing is an animal! To be more specific, it's a whole *colony* of animals—thousands all connected to form a single structure. The name *bryozoan* (pronounced bry-uh-ZO-an) means "moss animal." There have been bryozoans on Earth for about 480 million years. There are many species, but two you may find along the Pacific coast are the branched-spine bryozoan and the kelp encrusting bryozoan.

Close-up of the bryozoan's branched spines

Branched-Spine Bryozoan

(Flustrellidra corniculata)

APPEARANCE: Each individual creature—called a zooid (pronounced ZOH-oid)—is tiny, often less than a millimeter long. They all stick together in a much larger colony, though. The "spine" in their name doesn't refer to a backbone. These animals are invertebrates, which means they don't have one. The name refers to the tiny brown branched spines that stick out all over the colony, giving it a fuzzy appearance. The colonies look like a light brown plant with flat, fuzzy-looking leaves. Clumps of branched-spine bryozoan can grow to be 4 to 5 inches long.

FOOD: All bryozoans are filter feeders. They eat microscopic plankton floating in the water.

HABITAT: These creatures live in the low intertidal zone. That means you have the best chance of seeing them in tide pools during a minus tide. They often attach to kelp (seaweed). You can also sometimes find clusters mixed with seaweed along the wrack line after storms.

REPRODUCTION: Bryozoans reproduce in two ways: eggs and budding. They can spawn like fish by releasing eggs into the water. Those eggs hatch into larvae, which settle down after drifting for a while and become tiny new zooid. The second way is that zooids can sprout little copies of themselves (buds) that will grow into new zooids. Sometimes whole chunks of a colony will break off, float away, and reattach somewhere else.

RANGE: Found from Alaska to Southern California.

Kelp Encrusting Bryozoan
(Membranipora membranacea)

This is also known as a sea mat or kelp lace.

APPEARANCE: You could easily walk by this animal colony on the beach and assume it's just mold on rotting kelp, if you notice it at all. But get closer—really, really close. This is one of the times you'll want a magnifying glass or a camera that

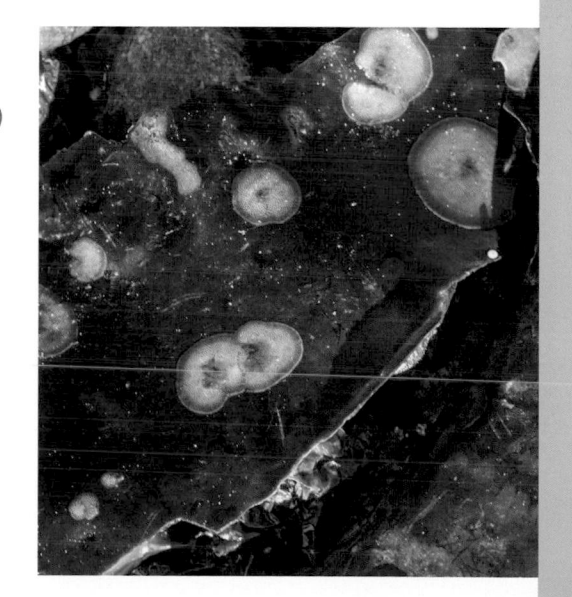

lets you zoom in. Those small (maybe an inch or two across), lacy white patches on the kelp are made up of cells like a honeycomb that each contain a separate zooid. Each patch is a whole community! When you zoom in, it's like looking into a whole new world.

FOOD: Kelp encrusting bryozoans are filter feeders.

HABITAT: Look for these bryozoans on the stipes (like leaves) of kelp that's washed up on the wrack line.

REPRODUCTION: These bryozoans reproduce by budding. The zooids sprout copies of themselves radiating outward in a sort of circle.

RANGE: Found from Alaska down to California (as well as on the Atlantic coast).

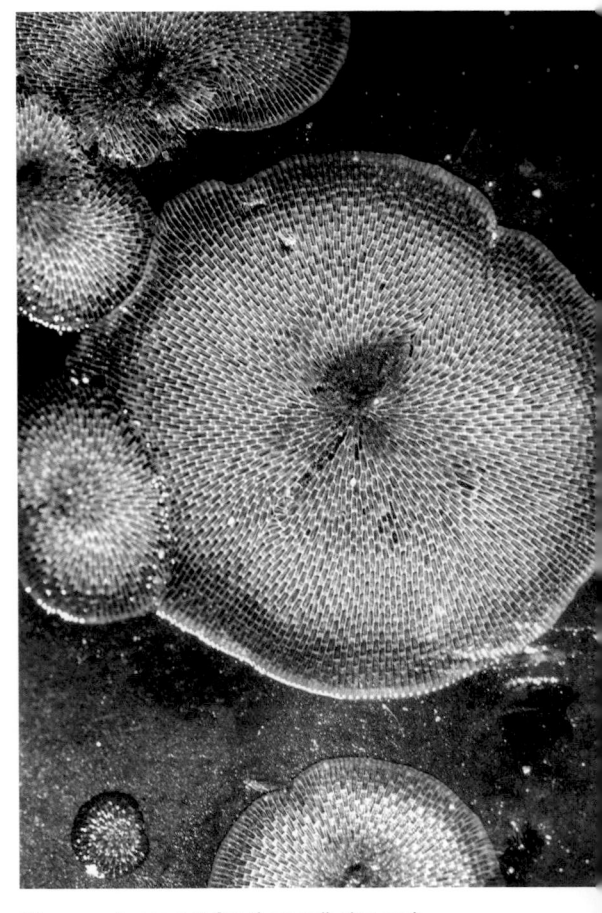

Close-up of a sea mat. See those cells that each hold a single zooid?

By-the-Wind Sailor

(Velella velella)

By-the-wind sailors look a bit like sea jellies (often called jellyfish; see page 135), but they aren't actually jellies. They're hydroids! Remember the tide pool hydroids from page 45? Well, here's one that spends its life floating around on the surface of the ocean. Like ostrich-plume hydroids, these "creatures" are each a whole community of tiny organisms living together as one being. Each individual organism (called a zooid) has a specific job to do for the community. Some zooids digest food while others catch prey or protect the colony.

If you look closely at the one in the middle, you can see that it's upside down with its tentacles showing.

APPEARANCE: By-the-wind sailors are deep blue and usually less than 2½ inches across. As their name suggests, they have a sail on top that lets them skim across the surface of the water pushed by the wind. On the underside, the colony has short tentacles a little like a sea jelly.

FOOD: These animals are carnivores, but the creatures they eat—zooplankton and fish eggs—are extremely small. Like other hydroids, they have stinging nematocysts on their tentacles that they use to stun their prey.

HABITAT: By-the-wind sailors float far out on the ocean. Since they are moved by the wind, though, it's common for them to be blown up onshore. Sometimes they come ashore by the hundreds or even thousands, and beachgoers can see (and smell) them all along the wrack line.

REPRODUCTION: By-the-wind sailors reproduce by budding. They break off little specially formed pieces of themselves to grow into a new hydroid colony.

RANGE: Found in oceans all over the world—look for them after big storms.

EGGS FROM THE DEEP!

Lucky beach explorers sometimes find fascinating signs of the life that dwells in the deep waters offshore.

These finger-length white pods are the egg sacs of an opalescent squid! Each sac can hold up to 300 squid eggs. The pods are laid on the ocean bottom, but it's not uncommon for storms to knock bundles loose and throw them up on the sand.

This leathery pouch has a great name: it's a mermaid's purse! Instead of holding spare change, though, this purse is home to a developing skate. When the skate is ready to hatch, it breaks through the pouch and swims away. Look for empty mermaid's purses up on the wrack line mixed in with washed-up seaweed.

Clam

A clam is a type of bivalve, which means "two shells." It has a pair of matching shells that are hinged on one side. Strong muscles let the clam open and close its shell to eat or protect itself from predators. Inside, the clam's squishy body has a large foot, which allows it to dig into the sand. You might also see the siphons—a pair of tubes that act kind of like a snorkel for the clam. One tube sucks water (including food and oxygen) into the clam. The other tube squirts water (and waste) out of the clam. The deeper a clam buries itself in the mud or sand, the longer its siphon will be.

Check out the water rushing out of this buried clam siphon! You can often tell when you're walking through an area with buried clams when you feel one squirt you in the leg.

There are over 15,000 species of clams worldwide. Some live in saltwater oceans and bays. Others live in freshwater rivers and lakes.

Clam shells may be smooth, or they may have striking patterns. Some have concentric rings, called that because they share the same center point.

APPEARANCE: Clams on the Pacific coast range from 2–inch (or smaller) littlenecks to giant geoducks (pronounced GOO-ee-ducks), which can have a shell around 8 inches across and a siphon up to 3 feet long. All clams have two shells joined by a hinge.

FOOD: Clams are filter feeders that eat plankton. They are also themselves an important food source for lots of predators, including snails, otters, birds, crabs, and humans.

HABITAT: Clams often live along sandy or muddy areas of the beach. They dig down—some just a couple of inches below the sand or mud and others, like the geoduck, as far down as they can go and still have their long siphons reach the surface. You can often find clam shells along the wrack line.

Clams may also have radiating ridge lines—like sunbeams that shoot out from a bump near the hinge called the umbo. See the radiating lines on this heart cockle clam?

REPRODUCTION: Clams hatch from eggs into larvae that float around as plankton until they settle to the bottom to develop into a clam.

RANGE: Found from Alaska down at least through Central California.

Species to Look For

HEART COCKLE *(Clinocardium nuttallii)*
Cockles are usually a mottled light brown, sometimes with a pinkish or peachy cast. They can be up to 5 inches across, but they're often much smaller. If you turn a cockle sideways, the two valves look like a heart!

See the heart shape? Look at the photo at the top of the page to see a heart cockle shell from the front.

PACIFIC LITTLENECK

(Leukoma staminea)

This little clam can live over ten years in the wild! It grows to about 2½ inches across and is often even smaller. It can be a lot of different colors—mostly creams, browns, and grays—and a variety of patterns (or none at all).

PACIFIC RAZOR CLAM

(Siliqua patula)

Razor clams are long and narrow, with a brownish shell up to 7½ inches long. The common name comes from the fact that early naturalists thought its shell looked like a closed straight razor. That's an old-fashioned razor that could fold into its handle.

ROUGH PIDDOCK *(Zirfaea pilsbryi)*

Peekaboo! Is that a clam down in that rock hole? The rough piddock is a type of boring clam, but that doesn't mean it's uninteresting. In this case, the word *boring* means drilling a hole through something. This type of clam bores right into rock using special spikes called shell teeth. Look for them inside round holes in large rocks or cliffsides.

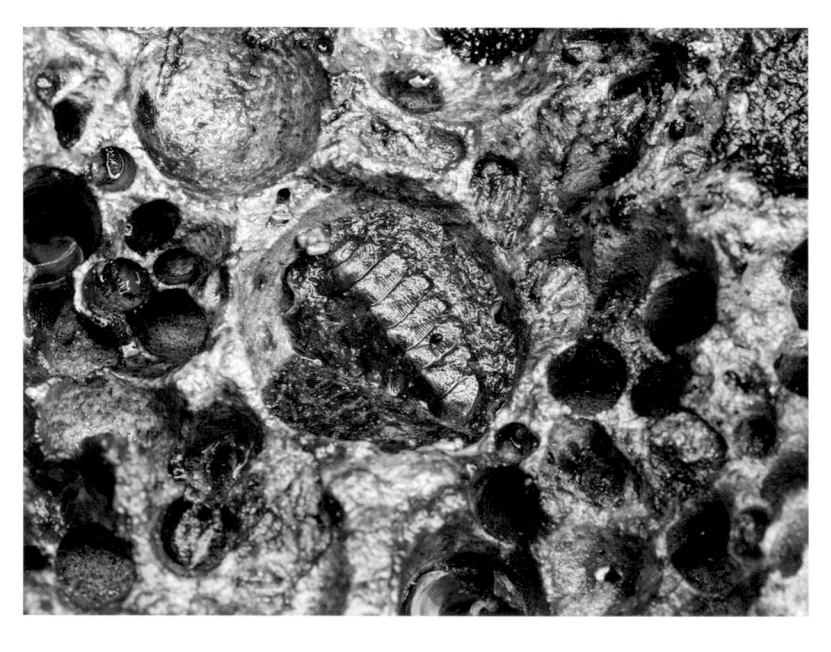

Who knew? After a piddock dies, its hole remains to provide shelter for all kinds of other creatures. It's like how the holes chiseled into trees by woodpeckers provide homes for different animals and birds on land. Check empty clam holes for chitons, limpets, crabs, and snails.

WHAT IS A RED TIDE?

Some types of algae produce toxins (poisons). Those toxins are usually not a problem because they're in super small amounts. But if the weather gets extra warm or there are more nutrients in the water than normal, those algae can bloom (reproduce quickly). When too many of certain algae are in the water, the toxins they produce can build up enough to make people and animals sick.

Shellfish, such as clams, are filter feeders. They suck up and filter anything good *or* bad out of the water. That means that if harmful toxins are floating around, they will be collected by the shellfish. Because of that, there are times when shellfish are too full of toxins for people and animals to safely eat. Scientists monitor the water and put out alerts when levels are dangerous.

Some types of algae will turn the water different colors, including red, so people sometimes call toxic algae blooms red tides. But not all red tides are toxic, and not all toxic tides are red (or any color at all). That's why scientists refer to the toxic tides as harmful algae blooms (or HABs) instead of "red tides."

Isopod

Isopods are crustaceans, which means they're distant relatives of crabs and shrimp. They have jointed legs and a hard exoskeleton (shell). There are over 10,000 species of isopods in the world, including the roly-poly bug you may have seen near your home. Different isopods live everywhere, from the oceans to the mountains.

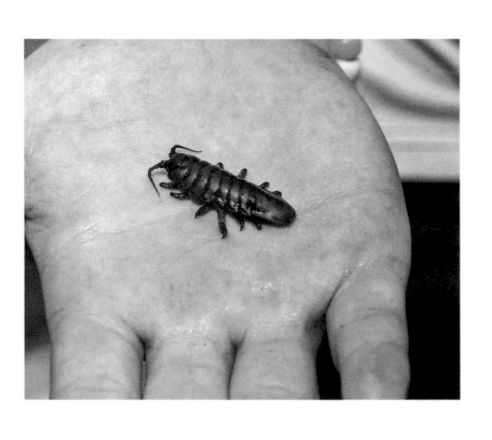

Who knew? Each segment of an isopod's body has a pair of legs called pleopods. Isopods don't just use these legs for walking and swimming: they also use them to breathe. Many beach creatures breathe through their legs or feet!

Kelp Isopod

(Pentidotea wosnesenskii)

APPEARANCE: This isopod is long and narrow, growing to about 1½ inches long. They are often green, but their color can be affected by the type of algae they eat. That means they can range from green or brown to purple or reddish.

Kelp isopods come in a range of colors, from greenish to reddish.

FOOD: Kelp isopods eat algae. They are themselves eaten by birds, fish, and other intertidal hunters. That makes them an important part of the food chain.

HABITAT: These creatures can often be found in or near kelp beds. They also live on rocks near mussel beds.

REPRODUCTION: Isopods hatch from eggs that are carried by the mother in a special pouch on her underside. Unlike many shore creatures, they hatch looking like tiny versions of their parents.

RANGE: Found from Alaska down to Central California.

Rock Louse

(Ligia pallasii)

This creature is also commonly called a sea slater.

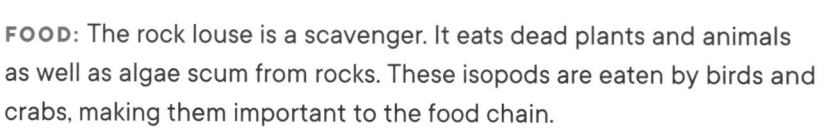

APPEARANCE: This isopod grows to a little more than an inch long. It has a wide, flat, segmented body that is dark brownish and blends well with cave walls. You could be walking right next to or under one and not even know it! They don't bite, though, and they're way more afraid of people than we are of them.

FOOD: The rock louse is a scavenger. It eats dead plants and animals as well as algae scum from rocks. These isopods are eaten by birds and crabs, making them important to the food chain.

HABITAT: These land creatures like to hang out near the sea, where they thrive in the cool, moist air. They can be found in caves or cracks in cliffs in the tidal area known as the spray zone, which is just above the high tide mark where waves still spray the rocks.

REPRODUCTION: The rock louse hatches from eggs that are carried by the mother in a special pouch on her underside.

RANGE: Found from Alaska to Central California.

Kelp

The Pacific coast is home to over thirty different species of kelp, which are like the trees of the ocean. Kelp is a kind of brown seaweed that grows close together, forming forests where many different organisms live and feed. Kelp forests create important ecosystems along the coast. Ocean creatures, marine mammals, and even birds use kelp forests for food and shelter. Some creatures eat the kelp itself; others eat the animals that live among its long stems.

APPEARANCE: Each variety of kelp is slightly different, so check out the details and photos on page 118 for clues to identify a few types. Kelp usually has a few basic parts: leaflike blades, a stemlike part called a stipe, and a holdfast that keeps them attached to the ocean floor. Since the blades are the part of the kelp that create energy from sunlight, it's important for them to be near the surface. They are held up by air-filled floats. Kelp grows really fast, sometimes up to 2 feet in a single day.

FOOD: Kelp produces its food through photosynthesis. Kelp is eaten by sea urchins, crabs, snails, and humans. Lots of different herbivores (plant eaters) graze on kelp. If something happens to the predators that normally hunt those herbivores and keep their numbers in check—things like overfishing or sea star wasting disease (see page 65)—the kelp-eating creatures can overgraze and destroy entire ecosystems. It's super important for coastlines to have hunters like sea stars and otters to keep everything in balance.

HABITAT: Since kelp uses sunlight to make food, it is found in water that is shallow enough to allow the sun to reach its leaflike blades.

REPRODUCTION: Kelp reproduce using microscopic spores, like ferns on land.

RANGE: Bull and five-ribbed kelp are found from Alaska to Southern California. Feather boa kelp can be found from British Columbia down to Baja California, Mexico. You can find sea palm from British Columbia to Central California.

Species to Look For

BULL KELP *(Nereocystis luetkeana)*
This is one of the largest kelp species in the world. It gets its common name from the fact that it looks like a bullwhip. Check out the long stipe topped by a hollow float and up to twenty blades. Bull kelp can be truly huge. The stipe can be over 100 feet long and the blades up to 15 feet long.

FEATHER BOA KELP *(Egregia menziesii)*
Squint your eyes a little. Can you see this as a feather boa—one of those fancy scarves you might wrap around your shoulders to play dress-up? That's what early naturalists saw when they made up the common name. These grow up to 35 feet long.

FIVE-RIBBED KELP *(Costaria costata)*
These are browner than some other types of kelp, and the blades are kind of puckered. Because of that, one of the other common names for this seaweed is seersucker kelp, after the wrinkly fabric. Each individual has a stipe attached to a single wrinkled blade divided lengthwise by five to seven ribs.

SEA PALM *(Postelsia palmaeformis)*
Check out this smallish kelp that looks like a palm tree! It only grows about 2 feet tall, and the blades are about 9 inches long.

Who knew? Not only does kelp provide a home for thousands of marine species, but it also helps fight climate change! Because kelp uses sunlight to make food out of carbon dioxide and water, it pulls carbon dioxide out of the ocean and releases oxygen, a process that is good for sea creatures and the planet as a whole.

Otter

Spotting an otter along the Pacific coast is always exciting. They're well known for being playful even after they're grown. If you're lucky, you'll get to watch them splash and dive or even catch a fish for dinner. Otters have fast metabolisms and need to eat a lot every day, so there's a good possibility you could see them on the hunt.

North American River Otter
(Lontra canadensis)

A lot of people think the only otters they'll see near the ocean are sea otters (see page 122), but river otters can be found in and near the ocean too. In fact, they're more common to spot along most beaches than sea otters. But they don't *always* live in or around the ocean. These otters also live around rivers and wetlands far inland from the coast.

APPEARANCE: These semiaquatic animals have bodies built for time in water and on land. They are long and sleek, reaching between 3 and 4 feet including their tail, which can be about a third of their entire length. River otters weigh between 10 and 30 pounds, with males growing larger than females. They have sleek brown fur and webbed feet. Their faces and bellies are lighter brown than their backs. Their long whiskers help them locate food in murky water.

FOOD: River otters are predators. Along the Pacific coast, they often dine on fish, crab, and birds' eggs. They may also nibble on aquatic plants or seaweed. All otters have sharp teeth and strong jaws to break through hard shells and bones.

HABITAT: River otters can live pretty much wherever there is water. They seek out spots with hollow logs or piles of large rocks because both offer places to stay cozy and hidden. But they prefer to have dens in burrows along the water so they can create an underwater entrance. They don't always dig their own, though. They often use abandoned homes made by nutria and beavers.

REPRODUCTION: Mother river otters raise litters of between one and three pups at a time in their dens. Pups are born with their eyes closed, and they don't learn to swim until they're about two months old.

RANGE: Found all along the Pacific coast of North America as well as near rivers and other wetlands across the continent.

Who knew? The easiest way to tell a river otter from a sea otter from the shore is to look at how it's swimming. Is it belly up or belly down? River otters swim tummy-side down, and usually climb out of the water to eat on the rocks. Sea otters float on their backs at the surface, especially when they're eating and resting.

Sea Otter

(Enhydra lutris)

All otters are mammals in the same family as weasels. That means they have hair, make milk to nurse their babies, and are warm-blooded. Only sea otters are considered marine mammals, though, which means they live pretty much all their lives in or around the ocean. This category includes seals, sea lions, whales, and dolphins. Unlike the other marine mammals, sea otters rely on their thick coats to keep warm, rather than blubber (body fat).

APPEARANCE: Sea otters are smaller than an average seal but two to three times as big as their river otter cousins. They can be up to 4 feet long (including tail) and weigh between 50 and 70 pounds. Their coats are made up of two different kinds of fur: a soft, warm undercoat like the down on a bird and a more waterproof outer coat made of guard hairs to keep their bodies dry in the cold ocean water. Sea otters have about a million hairs on every square inch of their bodies!

Sea otters are built for their watery life. Their rear feet are big and webbed for swimming, while their front paws have retractable claws for holding on to shells and slippery fish. This otter's tail is shorter and wider than its river cousin. Both its nostrils and its ears can be closed when diving underwater. Imagine having a self-plugging nose and ears when you swim!

Sea otters have the thickest fur of any animal on Earth. Back in the eighteenth and nineteenth centuries, people hunted sea otters for their fur. Sadly, they overhunted until almost none of the animals were left. Scientists estimate there were once nearly 300,000 sea otters in  the wild. By the early twentieth century, there were only between 1,000 and 2,000 individual sea otters left in all the world's oceans!

Sea otters are now protected by law, and their numbers have bounced back in most (but not all) of their range. The sea otter population is recovering in Alaska, California, Washington, and British Columbia. Seeing one along the Oregon coast is rare, but scientists are hoping to re-establish otter colonies there too.

As sea otter populations recover, humans need to be extra careful about ocean pollution that affects these creatures. Oil spills are especially harmful because oil keeps the otters' fur from trapping air that helps them float and stay warm in the cold waters of the Pacific.

FOOD: While river otters climb out on rocks to eat their meals (see page 120), sea otters eat floating on their backs. They also hunt in their own unique way. Sea otters will dive under the water for a few minutes at a time, turning over rocks on the ocean floor looking for prey like shellfish, crabs, and sea urchins.

Who knew? Sea otters have pockets in their coats! When a sea otter gathers food, it'll tuck the catch in a fold of loose skin under its arm and bring it back to the surface for eating. Some meals can be chomped through by the otter's strong teeth and jaws. With harder prey—like larger mussels and clams—sea otters may use a rock as a hammer to crack open the shell. It's one of a small group of animals other than humans that uses tools to eat.

HABITAT: Sea otters live almost entirely out in the ocean, rarely coming to shore. To stay safe, they often rest together in groups called rafts. Picture a giant raft made of between ten and a hundred sea otters all floating together out on the ocean. Sometimes they even hold hands to stay close! Another way they stay put is by wrapping themselves in kelp that's attached to the ocean floor.

REPRODUCTION: These are the only otters that give birth in the water. Mother sea otters will cuddle their single pup on their belly and spend hours every day grooming and fluffing it. That not only looks adorable, but is also super important for the safety of the pup. Baby sea otter fur is so fluffy and air-filled when it's well groomed that the pup will bob like a cork in the water. It's like they're wearing a full-body life jacket. When the mother needs to dive down to grab food, she may wrap her bobbing baby in kelp at the surface to keep it from floating away.

RANGE: Northern sea otters can be found from Alaska to Washington. A separate subspecies—southern sea otters—can be found in California.

Oyster

Several species of oysters live along the Pacific coast. Some regions and even particular bays have their own special variety. The native oyster along Pacific Northwest shores is the Olympia oyster (*Ostrea lurida*). Overharvesting and pollution have caused its population to fall over time, so people have brought in other species of oysters to raise for human food crops. One of the most common is a species from Japan called the Pacific oyster (*Magallana gigas*). A whole industry has built up around the farming of oysters.

APPEARANCE: Oysters are bivalve mollusks like clams, so they have two shells that close to protect their squishy body. Usually one of those shells will be permanently glued down to a rock or even another oyster. Olympia oysters grow to around 3½ inches long. If you find an oyster bigger than that, it's most likely a Pacific oyster,

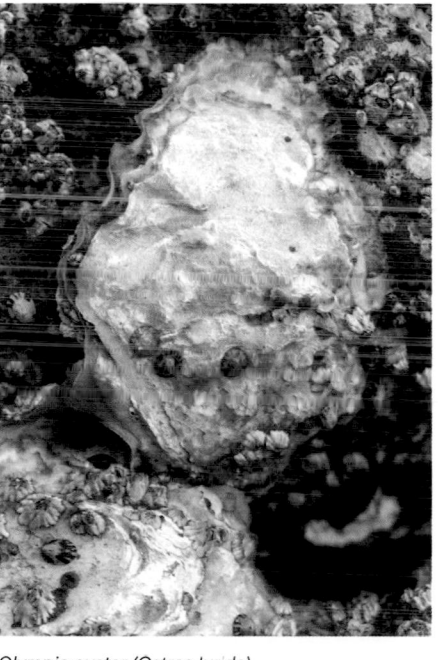

Olympia oyster (Ostrea lurida)

Pacific oyster (Magallana gigas)

which can grow to about 12 inches across. One of the reasons Pacific oysters are so often farmed is because they grow bigger in less time. Olympia oysters can be brownish gray to purplish black and are mostly round. Pacific oysters are long and narrow with a ruffled-looking edge.

FOOD: Oysters are filter feeders. They pull water in and filter the floating particles in it before letting it flow back out. Because of this, oysters are important cleaners in water ecosystems. But they are also at risk of gathering up a lot of toxins and pollution (see page 113). People who harvest oysters to eat pay close attention to the scientists who monitor the safety of the water.

Who knew? Have you ever had a rock in your shoe? Some species of oysters (and even some clams and mussels) have a cool trick for handling irritants like sand and tiny stones that get stuck inside their shell. They coat it with a substance called nacre (NAY-cur) and turn the annoying piece of sand into a pearl. Imagine your body making a gem out of something that was poking you!

Nacre—also called mother of pearl—is also used to make the shell. See the pearly white interior?

HABITAT: You can find both of these oysters in rock beds in the low (deeper) intertidal zone. They build on rocks and older shells, forming oyster beds. There are lots of different oyster farms throughout the Puget Sound and along the West Coast from British Columbia down to Central California.

REPRODUCTION: In the wild, these two oysters reproduce a bit differently from each other. The female native Olympia oyster carries

See the wavy edges of this bivalve's shell? That's how you can easily tell oysters from other shellfish along the coast.

fertilized eggs in a brooding chamber inside her shell until the little larvae are ready to head off and look for a place to glue themselves down permanently. The Pacific oyster spawns (releases its eggs) into the water. Fertilized eggs hatch into larvae that then find a place to settle down. On oyster farms, people order oyster "seeds" from breeders. The "seeds" are actually immature oysters just at the point when they're ready to stick themselves down. Farmers place each oyster seed on special underwater cages or other structures that keep them safe while growing.

RANGE: Olympia oysters can be found from Alaska down to Mexico. While Pacific oysters were originally from Japan, they are now being raised on farms all over the world and can be found locally from Alaska to California.

Pacific Mole Crab

(Emerita analoga)

Despite the name, this little creature isn't really a crab. It is a crustacean, though, so we can think of it as a crab cousin. Pacific mole crabs are more closely related to hermit crabs than true crabs.

APPEARANCE: Pacific mole crabs have a hard outer shell. They're kind of egg shaped and grow to be just under 1½ inches. The smooth shell is mostly sand colored (gray to light brown), which helps camouflage this animal along the beach. Mole crabs have five pairs of walking legs and three pairs of pleopods (swimming legs). They don't have any pincers like a true crab, and they can't bite you.

Pacific mole crab digging

FOOD: Pacific mole crabs are filter feeders who mostly eat detritus (pronounced dih-TRY-tus)—tiny floating bits of dead plant and animal matter. These creatures ride the water in after waves crash against the shore, then quickly dig backward into the sand so just their front end pokes out to feed. In fact, they always move backward, whether crawling, digging, or swimming. Pacific mole crabs are eaten by fish, seabirds, and other hungry predators.

HABITAT: These little creatures live in the sand along the swash zone—the part of the beach where the waves wash in.

REPRODUCTION: A female mole crab lays up to 45,000 eggs in a single batch! She carries the cluster of bright orange eggs on her abdomen until they hatch into swimming larvae. After several months, they settle onto the beach and transform into juvenile mole crabs.

RANGE: Found from Alaska to South America, but they are less common on the beaches of Washington than Oregon.

A mole crab climbs out of the sand, scurries over the surface, and then digs itself under again in a matter of seconds.

Rock

Animals and algae are fun to explore at the beach, but you also should check out the nonliving treasures along the coast. This area has some of the most interesting rocks around.

AGATE

Lots of beach explorers like to collect rocks and agates. Agates are a type of semiprecious stone that is translucent. That means light can pass through it. These pretty stones really stand out on the beach if you start watching for them. Agates comes in many colors, including red, orange, yellow, white, almost clear, and blue. They were formed millions of years ago inside empty spaces in volcanic rocks. Look for them in areas with gravel bars or wave-tumbled stones along the sand.

FOSSIL

While you're exploring the amazing wildlife along the beach, be sure to also keep an eye out for signs of life from long ago. If you look carefully in rocky areas, you may find fossils from around 30 million years ago! In some cases, you can see shells and bones encased in stone. You might also find shells that have been themselves slowly turned to stone as minerals replaced their original form over millions of years.

If you find a small, loose fossil, it's fine to take it home as a souvenir. But it's illegal to dig fossils out of cliffs or large rocks.

ROCK FORMATION

While you're checking out rocks, spend some time admiring the various beautiful formations that occur because of the amazing natural forces along the Pacific. Wind, waves, deposits of different minerals, and even the movement of the land itself can make coastal rocks into works of art.

SEA STACK

Sea stacks are the giants of the beach rocks. They were formed over millions of years as waves and weather eroded parts of beach cliffs away. Eventually the rocks left standing were surrounded by water, making them perfect islands for sea-birds and marine mammals

to safely raise their young away from predators on land or in the deep waters of the ocean.

Along with pretty agates and shells, lots of beachcombers collect pieces of sea glass. When regular glass ends up in the ocean, it gets tumbled against the rocks and sand, buffing off the sharp edges. The result is a smooth, rounded piece of glass that is a frosted version of its original color. Since glass is mostly made out of sand to start, the ground-off bits just go back to being sand again. In some ways, that makes glass different from other trash that washes up onshore. How do you think glass is different from plastic? In what ways could glass still be a problem on the coast?

Sand Dollar, Eccentric

(Dendraster excentricus)

Sand dollars are flatter cousins of sea urchins (see page 66). Their tests (shells) are often found along the sand. Lucky beach explorers can sometimes come across them whole, bleached white by the sun. Even luckier beachcombers will get a chance to see one of these creatures alive.

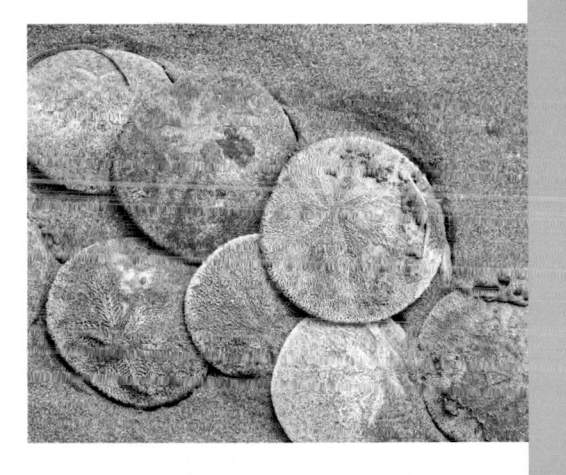

APPEARANCE: The common name "sand dollar" comes from the fact that these round beauties reminded early naturalists of a silver dollar coin. Living sand dollars can be a range of colors, including shades of gray, brown, and purple. Their entire body is covered with tiny movable spines. If you gently turn a live sand dollar over, you can see the spines moving in a ripple. They use those spines to move around, dig into the sand, bring food to their mouth,

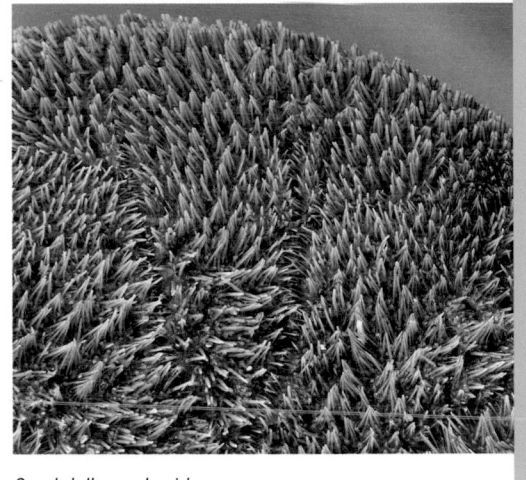

Sand dollar underside

and even to breathe. The spines up on top of the test act as gills! Sand dollars can grow as large as 3 inches across. The topside of the test has what looks like a five-petaled flower on it.

Who knew? The flower shape on the top of the eccentric sand dollar is off-center. That's how scientists chose the *excentricus* part of the name. People sometimes use the word *eccentric* to describe a person who is maybe a little odd, but in a good way. In science, it means a little off-center, like the flower on the sand dollar shell.

FOOD: Sand dollars bury one end in the sand and tip their body up to catch small prey such as plankton, detritus, and algae floating in the water. Their mouth—like the sea urchin—is on the underside of the test. Sand dollars are eaten by some fish, crabs, and gulls.

HABITAT: Sand dollars live underwater near the shore along the coast as well as in inlets and bays. They live so close together that there can be hundreds of sand dollars in a single square meter of

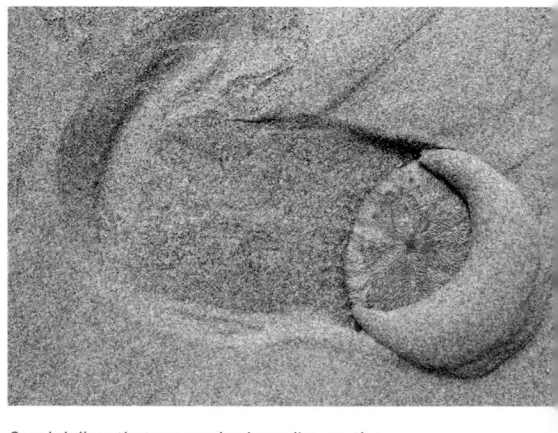

Sand dollars that are washed up alive on the shore may try to bury themselves in the sand for protection. Can you see how this one is pushing itself under the sand with its little spines?

sand! Sometimes for reasons nobody really understands, thousands of live sand dollars will beach themselves all at once.

REPRODUCTION: Sand dollars spawn (release eggs) into the water. The eggs, which are small and orange, have a thick coating on them to prevent adult sand dollars from eating them. That's a good thing since they feed on tiny eggs and other little things floating in the water. The eggs hatch out as larvae, which float around for up to several months before settling down to become a tiny sand dollar.

RANGE: Found from Alaska to Baja California, Mexico.

Sea Jelly

Lots of people call this a jellyfish, but just like the sea star (starfish), this animal is not a fish. Instead, it belongs to a big group of animals called Cnidaria (pronounced nigh-DARE-ee-uh) that has been on Earth for over 600 million years.

Be careful when you investigate these creatures. Some can sting even after they're washed up on the shore.

Who knew? Sea jellies are made up of mostly water, but they're still living animals and are distantly related to anemones. They don't have a heart, lungs, or even a brain, but they do have a nervous system—the simplest one in the animal kingdom. It's basically a web of nerves that allow jellies to sense movement as well as to squeeze their body to move. Even though that technically lets them swim, they aren't strong enough to resist the current. Since they mostly flow with the water, they're considered zooplankton, even though they're much larger than most plankton.

APPEARANCE: Most sea jellies have a translucent (lets light through) or transparent (clear) body called a hood or a bell because of its shape. They have thin stinging tentacles trailing down from around the bottom edge of the bell. Sea jellies also have wider structures called oral arms hanging down around the mouth in the middle of the bell. Think of the oral arms like long fluffy lips. The jelly uses them to bring food to its mouth.

Medusa (pronounced meh-DOO-suh) is a famous monster from Greek mythology who had snakes on her head instead of hair. Picture a sea jelly with its long waving tentacles. Early naturalists saw that and thought of the mythical

Medusa. Several types of sea creatures go through what is called a medusa phase in their life cycle, where they have a bell-shaped body and hairlike tentacles.

FOOD: Sea jellies have stinging nematocysts on their tentacles like those found in sea anemones. They sting their prey—usually zooplankton or even other jellies—and use their oral arms to bring the food to their digestion cavity.

HABITAT: Sea jellies drift with the currents in the ocean. You can often find them washed up along sandy beaches, especially after a storm. *Caution:* Unlike many beach creatures, some sea jellies can painfully sting humans, some even after they're dead and washed up onshore. Be very careful when checking out these fascinating animals.

REPRODUCTION: What we picture as a sea jelly is actually the medusa stage (see sidebar) of a creature that looks very different at various points in its life. Sea jellies release eggs into the water that hatch into larvae. Each larva settles on a rock, the seafloor, or even a manmade pier and becomes a polyp that looks like a tiny anemone. That polyp then creates buds that eventually break off and float away to become more sea jellies.

RANGE: All of the jellies described in this book can be found from Alaska to Southern California (and a few even farther south).

Species to Look For

LION'S MANE JELLY *(Cyanea capillata)*
This sea jelly can be huge—normally around 20 inches across with tentacles around 10 feet long. Sometimes, though, they can be as big as 8 feet across with tentacles over 100 feet long! Imagine coming across something that huge out in the water!

PACIFIC MOON JELLY *(Aurelia labiata)*
These are smaller than lion's mane jellies, only growing to about 16 inches across. They can still be impressive finds along the sand, though. The reproductive organs are visible through the translucent body—check out the four purple blobs at their center.

PACIFIC SEA NETTLE (*Chrysaora fuscescens***)**

This jelly is amber colored with tentacles around its bell. It also has long, frilly oral arms that help it move captured prey to its mouth. It grows up to 17 inches across, and its oral arms can be up to 15 feet long. The photo here of it swimming was taken at an aquarium, so you can see the tentacles and oral arms. On the sand, they most often look like a golden blob.

Along with the Cnidaria sea jellies (the "true jellies"), there are also a few other groups of similar creatures in the ocean from totally different branches of the animal kingdom. That includes this crystal jelly (*Aequorea victoria*). This jelly is bioluminescent, which means when it's poked it can flash a blue-green light!

Sea Lion

This huge marine mammal looks a lot like its cousin, the harbor seal (see page 139). How will you ever tell them apart? They're both pinnipeds (pronounced PIN-I-peds), which means "fin-footed," but there are some key differences you can spot.

Juvenile and female Steller sea lions

First, look at the flippers. Sea lions have big front and back flippers they can use to walk on land. Harbor seals have smaller flippers, and they have to kind of belly crawl on land. Second, look at the ears. Can you see a little flap, or is there just a hole? Sea lions have a visible ear flap, but harbor seals don't. Third, listen. Is the creature barking loudly and making a lot of noise? That's a sea lion. Seals are much quieter. You'll probably only hear a grunt or snort, if anything.

California sea lions

APPEARANCE: Sea lions have short brownish fur and broad chests. There are two different species of sea lions that live along the Pacific coast. The first (and largest) is the Steller sea lion (*Eumetopias jubatus*), which was named after Georg Steller, the same naturalist who named our local Steller's jays. Male Steller sea lions can weigh up to 2,500 pounds—that's more than a ton! Females can weigh up to 1,000 pounds. The second species is the California sea lion (*Zalophus californianus*).

California sea lions are much smaller than their Steller cousins. Males can weigh around 1,100 pounds and have a noticeable ridge on their forehead, while females are a petite 220 pounds. Steller sea lions' fur is a lighter brown than the California variety, except for their pups, who are a darker brown until about six months old. One last way to tell the two species apart is to listen. California sea lions bark loudly, while Steller sea lions growl!

FOOD: Sea lions eat many different types of fish and other sea animals (such as octopus). They are mammals, so babies are nursed when they're young.

HABITAT: Sea lions need water for fishing as well as protected dry land for giving birth and resting. The places they give birth are called rookeries—a name also used for bird nesting colonies. Other places where they pull themselves from the water to rest and sunbathe are called haulouts. Look for sea lions on rocks, sandy beaches, and manmade docks—sometimes even far upriver from the coast if there are fish to be caught.

REPRODUCTION: During the summer, sea lion females give birth on land to a single pup at a time. The mother will alternate nursing the baby and swimming off to hunt and forage for herself. Because of this, spotting sea lion pups alone on the shore is completely normal. If you see a baby sea lion or other marine mammal on the beach, please give it space. If it seems to be in distress, call a local wildlife rescue. *Never approach any marine mammal on your own.*

Sea lion eating an octopus. It was quite a battle!

Young Steller sea lion

RANGE: Steller sea lions mostly live in the North Pacific, but their range extends down to Central California. Male California sea lions migrate up to Alaska from their breeding grounds ranging from Southern California down to Central Mexico. Females of the species usually stay near the breeding colonies. They can sometimes be seen as far north as Oregon and Washington in years when the water is warmer.

MARINE MAMMAL PROTECTION ACT

Since 1972 all marine mammals in the United States have been legally protected from being hunted or harassed. Give marine mammals *lots* of space every day, plus extra when you see babies. You don't want to scare these animals and accidentally separate a mother from her pup. Be sure to always keep dogs on a leash when you're on a beach with seals, sea lions, otters, or similar wildlife—even if you think your dog will be fine. Other guidelines to follow:

- Stay at least 50 yards away from marine mammals on land. (That's half of a football field.)
- Do not take selfies with them from any closer than 50 yards. It's illegal and dangerous.
- Do not offer these animals food of any kind.

All of the marine mammal images in this book were taken with a long telephoto lens and then cropped. Even serious photographers must give these animals their space.

If you ever come across a marine mammal that seems to be in trouble—stranded up on the beach, caught in trash like fishing line, or appearing sick or injured—contact the US Fish and Wildlife Service (1-800-344-9453) or a local marine mammal rehabilitation and protection group.

Seal, Harbor

(Phoca vitulina)

Harbor seals are one of the most common marine mammals seen along the coast. They spend about half of their time resting on rocks and beaches out of the water. That gives beachgoers a good chance to spot them. Seals normally only dive for a few

minutes at a time. But if they want to, they can stay underwater up to 30 minutes!

Check out the claws on this guy! Seals may look cute, but they're carnivores.

APPEARANCE: Adult harbor seals are between 5 and 6 feet long and weigh up to 285 pounds. Males are a bit larger than females. They have short flippers that help them swim but aren't great for moving around on land. They have arm and leg bones, but the only part that sticks out beyond their torso is basically their hands and feet. Picture trying to walk if you could only move your feet and not your entire leg. Because of that, seals sort of belly crawl like a caterpillar when they're out of the water.

Unlike sea lions, harbor seal ears are hidden, showing as just a hole on either side of their heads. Their fur varies in color from tan to gray with light or dark spots. They have long, sensitive whiskers on their face that help them sense fish and other prey in the water.

Who knew? Each seal whisker has over 1,500 nerves at its base, and seals can have up to fifty whiskers. That makes for a supersensitive snout! Seals can sense the size and shape of a fish underwater more than a hundred feet away!

FOOD: Harbor seals are predators that eat fish, crabs, shellfish, and other crustaceans. They don't need to drink water because they get all the water they need from their food. When seals nurse their young, their milk is almost 50 percent fat! Compare that to the 2 percent milk you may have had on your cereal this morning. Fat is necessary for seals to maintain the thick layer of blubber (body fat) that keeps them warm and helps them float in the cold ocean water.

HABITAT: Like sea lions, harbor seals need access to both water and land (or drifting sea ice) so they can hunt and haul out to rest.

Harbor seal nose-to-nose with a pup

REPRODUCTION: Harbor seals usually give birth between February and July in rookeries similar to their sea lion cousins. Along the beaches of California, they have their pups earlier than they do in the colder north. Pups are born on land but are able to swim right away. After just a couple of days, they can already dive for a minute or two at a time.

RANGE: Found from Alaska down to Baja California, Mexico.

Shrimp

A shrimp is a type of crustacean related to crabs and barnacles. Many (including those described here) are also part of a group called decapods, which literally means "ten legs." It's not actually that simple, though. Lots of shrimp do have ten skinny legs for walking. They also have some shorter "legs" (called swimmerets) for swimming. Shrimp also use their muscular tails to get an extra quick boost (usually backward) when they're in the water.

The Pacific coast has hundreds of species of shrimp and shrimplike creatures, each with their own look and size. Some are only about ½ inch long, while others are as large as 9 inches from head to tail. They all have a hard outer shell, an elongated body, and long antennae. Some also have enlarged front legs ending in pincers.

Bay Ghost Shrimp
(Neotrypaea californiensis)

APPEARANCE: This type of shrimp grows up to around 4½ inches long and can be a wide range of colors, from orange or pink to off-white. One of its claws is much bigger than the other, especially on the males.

FOOD: Ghost shrimp feed on the tiny floating stuff in the water, both detritus (tiny bits of dead matter) and plankton. They gather it while staying safely burrowed

under the sand or mud and collecting food in the sediment. Ghost shrimp are eaten by lots of larger predators, including several species of shorebirds. They are also dug up and used by human fishers as bait.

Bay ghost shrimp burrow: look for a mound with a hole in the middle.

HABITAT: These creatures live on sandy beaches and mudflats in the middle to low intertidal zone—closer to the water rather than way up on dry sand. They spend their time under the surface of the sand digging tunnels. You are more likely to spot the entrance and exit holes than you are the shrimp themselves. Their burrows look like short mounds with a hole in the center.

REPRODUCTION: Female ghost shrimp carry their eggs on their abdomen for several months. Then, usually in the middle of the summer, the eggs hatch into larvae. The larvae float around as plankton for up to eight weeks, changing and growing until they return to the shore and make one final transition into a ghost shrimp.

RANGE: Found from Alaska to Baja California, Mexico.

Smooth Bay Shrimp
(Lissocrangon stylirostris)

APPEARANCE: This shrimp has an exoskeleton that looks just like the sand where it lives. The light background is speckled with brown and black, camouflaging the smooth bay shrimp perfectly. It can dig straight down and bury itself almost instantly if it wants to hide. At only about 2½ inches long, these are smaller than their ghost shrimp cousins.

FOOD: The smooth bay shrimp is an ambush predator. It hides in the sand to catch tiny fish and isopods. It is also food for lots of animals and birds. Humans sometimes use these shrimp for bait if they can find them. It's not easy to do with that amazing camouflage!

HABITAT: These shrimp live along the sandy shore, especially near or in the wrack line.

REPRODUCTION: Like many other shrimp, smooth bay shrimp females carry their eggs on their abdomen for several months. The eggs hatch and then go through a few different larval forms before returning to the shore to make one final change into an adult.

RANGE: Found from Alaska to Baja California, Mexico.

Surfgrass

Surprise! This isn't seaweed. It's a flowering plant—one of very few that live in salt water. Several different species of surfgrasses live along the Pacific coast, including Scouler's surfgrass (*Phyllospadix scouleri*), Torrey's surfgrass (*Phyllospadix torreyi*), and common eelgrass (*Zostera marina*).

APPEARANCE: Surfgrass looks a lot like land-based grasses, because it *is* like them other than the fact that it lives in water. It is long, flat, and tapers to a pointed tip. Different species can have grass blades ranging from 3 feet to around 10 feet long. That's some long grass!

FOOD: Surfgrasses make their own food through photosynthesis. They take in sunlight and carbon dioxide and create oxygen and sugar. Like kelp forests, these grasses provide food and shelter for a wide range of ocean creatures.

HABITAT: Surfgrass can be found along the shallow parts of the coastal waters growing from rocks or mud. It forms meadows, providing important habitat for many different marine animals such as fish, crabs, nudibranchs, and shrimp.

REPRODUCTION: Like land plants, surfgrasses reproduce by making seeds. Some species even make seeds that humans have eaten like other grains.

RANGE: Various forms of surfgrasses live all along the Pacific coast from Alaska to Southern California.

WHALES

Along the Pacific, these majestic, intelligent giants often travel fairly close to shore, especially when they have babies (calves) with them. That means you have a good chance of spotting them from the beach! How is that possible with such a huge ocean to scan? You just have to know what to look for.

A whale is a mammal that breathes air just like you do. Its nostrils, called a blowhole, are located on the back of its head. When it goes underwater, the blowhole closes to keep the water out. When it surfaces, a huge puff of warm whale breath comes out of the blowhole and immediately turns to visible steam, like what happens when you breathe out on a cold day. That steam cloud is called a blow or a spout, which you can search for from the shore.

Other signs to look for are flukes (whale tail fins) or flippers (whale hands) as swimming giants roll over or dive in the sunshine. To spot orcas (killer whales), look for their giant dorsal (back) fins—some are over 5 feet tall!

If you're really lucky, you may see the most amazing whale behavior of all: a breach. When a whale breaches, it propels itself out of the water and crashes down on its side in a giant splash of seawater. Keep your eyes open!

Shorebirds

The Pacific coastline teems with shorebirds that thrive in the salty, windy, watery world of the ocean's edge. In some ways, they're a lot like the backyard birds you see every day. But they also have adaptations that let them thrive where other animals couldn't. An adaptation is something about an animal—either a body feature or how it behaves—that helps it survive. Some of these birds live on the coast year-round. Others spend most of their lives out on the open waters of the ocean, only coming to shore when it's time to lay eggs. Each bird has developed ways to prosper in some of the harshest conditions on Earth.

Who knew? Birds hatch out of their eggs looking one of two basic ways. Some chicks hatch with their eyes closed and are mostly naked and helpless. Scientists call birds like that altricial (pronounced al-TRISH-ul). Altricial birds stay in the nest for weeks, relying on their parents for everything, including food and warmth. Other chicks hatch out covered in fluffy down with their eyes open. Those are called precocial birds (pronounced pre-COE-shull). Have you ever heard the word *precocious* used to describe a kid who's really advanced? These "advanced" chicks are ready to go exploring right from the start.

Cormorant

Cormorants are waterbirds with a long snaky neck, a thin hooked bill, and a fanned tail. They swim low in the water with their tails extended behind them and their heads raised. Picture a black goose starting to submerge like a submarine—it's a little like that.

Three species of cormorants are often found along the West Coast: Brandt's, double-crested, and pelagic. It is not uncommon to see all three near each other.

Brandt's Cormorant
(Urile penicillatus)

The name of this Pacific coastal cormorant comes from a German naturalist who didn't actually see one in the wild. His name was Johann Friedrich von Brandt, and he examined specimens of this bird brought to him while he worked at a museum in Russia during the 1800s.

APPEARANCE: Brandt's cormorants are the largest of the Pacific coast cormorant species. They're around 34 inches long and have a wingspan of about 48 inches. These birds are mostly black with bright blue eyes. During breeding season, they also have stunning bright blue throat feathers. The blue throat is the easiest way to pick out an adult Brandt's cormorant from a distance. Juveniles are a soft grayish brown.

A nesting pair of Brandt's cormorants

FOOD: Cormorants eat fish, diving to catch their prey. They use their feet and sometimes their wings to propel themselves through the water. Brandt's cormorants can dive up to 150 feet deep in search of prey.

HABITAT: Brandt's cormorants only live along the coast. They're almost never seen inland and rarely even fly over dry land. You can spot these large birds roosting (settling down for sleep) and resting on cliffs and rocks as well as on human structures near water. They live in large colonies with other cormorants and various shorebirds.

REPRODUCTION: Brandt's cormorants build nests of eelgrass, algae, sticks, and other natural material on the sloped side of a cliff, often in the same spot as the previous year. They glue it all to the hillside with their own poop, called guano (pronounced GWAH-no). You use what you have! The female lays between one and six eggs, and the chicks hatch out naked and helpless (altricial).

RANGE: This bird is a year-round resident from Baja California, Mexico, up through southern British Columbia. They can also be seen farther north to Alaska and farther south to Central Mexico in the winter months. They tend to follow the California Current, which brings cold water down the coast from Alaska, bringing small cold-water fish such as anchovies and sardines for them to eat.

Double-Crested Cormorant

(Nannopterum auritum)

All cormorants are excellent swimmers, but unlike ducks, whose outer feathers are waterproof, cormorants have feathers that let water soak in so they can dive more easily. Some species—including the double-crested cormorant—have a striking way of drying off after they come out of the water. They stand upright with their wings extended out to the side as their feathers dry in the sun. That posture is a great way to recognize this cormorant from a distance.

APPEARANCE: This species is brownish black all over with a stunning brown-and-black pattern on its wing feathers. They have an orange patch of skin where their bill meets their face, and during breeding season they sport tufts of white or black feathers on either side of their head (their double crests). This cormorant's eyes can be so brightly turquoise blue that they look like jewels. If you get a chance to peek, the inside of its mouth is blue as well!

FOOD: Cormorants are fish eaters, diving to catch their prey. The hook at the end of their bill helps with holding on to their slippery meals. If a fish is large, the cormorant may flip it around so it can be swallowed headfirst.

HABITAT: The double-crested cormorant is different from the other two types because it can often be found inland around freshwater lakes and rivers as well as on the coast. Since it's a swimming, fish-eating bird, it always needs to live in and around water. It just doesn't care if the water is salty or not.

REPRODUCTION: Double-crested cormorants nest on the ground as well as in trees. They lay between one and seven eggs per clutch (a group laid together). The babies are born naked and helpless (altricial).

RANGE: Found throughout most of North America, especially along the coasts.

Pelagic Cormorant
(Urile pelagicus)

The word *pelagic* in the name of this cormorant means "relating to the open sea." It's not super accurate in this case, though, since this bird never goes very far from shore.

APPEARANCE: This is the smallest of the Pacific cormorants and has a thinner neck than the others. These birds are blackish all over, but in breeding season their feathers turn iridescent, meaning they shine purple and green in the light. They also have reddish skin right around their bills and

Baby pelagic cormorants waiting for a meal.

large white patches on their flanks (the sides of their body under the wings).

FOOD: Like the other birds in this group, pelagic cormorants eat fish, diving deep underwater to catch their prey.

HABITAT: Like the Brandt's, this is only a coastal bird. It stays near the shore and around islands.

REPRODUCTION: Because it's the smallest cormorant, the pelagic can build its nests on steeper cliffs and smaller ledges than the others. They build nests of grass, seaweed, sticks, and other material on cliffs or abandoned human structures. They glue it all together with their guano. They lay between one and eight eggs per clutch, and the babies are born naked and helpless.

RANGE: Found year-round from Alaska down to Central California. In the winter, they go as far south as Baja California, Mexico, chasing prey.

Crow, American

(Corvus brachyrhynchos)

Many people think of crows as inland birds, but they're an important part of the coastal ecosystem as well. One type of crow commonly seen along the beaches of Washington, Alaska, and British Columbia was considered its own species until the summer of 2020, when the American Ornithological Society (the bird scientist group that decides these things) regrouped the

Northwestern crow to be part of the American crow species. Scientists change categories and names as they learn more about an animal.

Crows belong to a smart, curious group of birds called corvids. In the fall and winter, crows come together in massive roosting flocks that can have tens of thousands of birds.

APPEARANCE: The coastal crows in the Pacific Northwest are usually a bit smaller than their inland cousins, which is one reason they used to be considered their own species. All crows are still impressively large, though, with bodies 16 to 21 inches long and a wingspan of 34 to 39 inches. Crows are black all over, including their beaks and legs. Even their brown eyes are so dark they look black from a distance. In fact, crows and ravens are the only all-black birds in North America. All other "blackbirds" have some other color somewhere—on their beaks, legs, or feathers.

FOOD: Crows are opportunistic feeders, which means they will eat whatever they can find, plant or animal. On the coast (including the Puget Sound and other inlets and bays), that means they will take advantage of the delicious food along the wrack line, such as small fish and dead crabs.

HABITAT: Crows will live anywhere with trees or structures to perch on and available food. The beaches along the coast provide both. In addition to seeing these birds out on the sand, you are likely to find them around parking lots looking for fallen snacks from human picnickers.

REPRODUCTION: Crow couples build their nests together out of sticks and twigs. The size of the nest can range from as small as 6 inches to as large as 18 inches across. The eggs are pale blue-green, and the babies hatch out naked except for little tufts of gray down. Crows have strong family groups along with their larger flocks. Offspring often stay around their parents for the first couple of years and help care for future broods.

RANGE: Found year-round from Alaska down to Southern California.

Adult crow feeding a fledgling. Can you see the pink at the base of the baby's beak? That's a good way to spot a baby from a distance.

Eagle, Bald

(Haliaeetus leucocephalus)

You may not think of bald eagles as beach birds, but the Pacific coast is a perfect environment for these majestic raptors (birds of prey). Tall trees and cliffs? Check! Water with an assortment of fish and other delicious snacks? Check! In fact, bald eagles are super common along West Coast beaches. As you're walking along the sand, look up along the shore away from the water

and toward the very tops of trees. Also, pay attention to other birds, especially gulls. They'll often get frantic when there's an eagle around.

APPEARANCE: Bald eagles are one of the largest birds in North America. They range from 28 to 39 inches long, with a wingspan over 6½ feet. As with other birds of prey, the female is usually bigger than the male. All raptors have large, sharp talons on their feet and hooked beaks that they use to grab and tear their food. The talons and beaks on eagles are some of the sharpest and most powerful in the animal kingdom.

Adult bald eagles have a classic white head and dark brown body. Juveniles are streaked brown all over. It takes eagles up to five years to reach their adult form, so don't just look for that white head. Brown-all-over birds on the beach could be eagles too!

FOOD: Bald eagles really like fish, but they'll hunt and eat whatever is available with the least amount of effort. For example, they'll often steal other animals' prey or eat the flesh from dead animals (carrion) they find lying on the ground. At the beach, their meal might include young seabirds.

At the beach, bald eagles eat fish as well as unlucky sea birds like this one.

HABITAT: Bald eagles like tall trees or dead snags near bodies of water. They thrive all along the Pacific coast and are sometimes even spotted down on the sand or on rocky beaches.

REPRODUCTION: Bald eagles build what may be the largest nests in the world. Made mostly of sticks, these giant homes are placed high up in the top of the tallest evergreen trees. The nests can be 2 to 4 feet deep and 4 to 6 feet wide on average. Eagles often return to the same nest year

Juvenile bald eagle with a tiny fish snack

after year, and they add on to the nest when they do. Researchers have found nests as big as 9 feet across! Bald eagles lay one to three eggs per clutch once a year. The babies—called eaglets—hatch out covered in gray fuzzy down.

RANGE: Bald eagles are common year-round residents from Alaska to Northern California. In the winter months, they can be found down to Southern California.

Gull

Many people call these seagulls because they're so common near the ocean. The more accurate term is just plain *gulls*, but they really are everywhere along the coast There are more than fifty different species of gulls in the world. If you want to try to tell them apart, compare the details, including bill color, leg color, eye color, wing markings, and other slight differences. This can be challenging even for experienced birders, so be patient. Even within a single species, a gull can look completely different on its way from baby to adult. Also, multiple species of gulls often crossbreed, so there are

lots of birds with characteristics of more than one species.

Sometimes the tracks on the beach—like these gull tracks—can tell a whole story that you might have otherwise missed.

APPEARANCE: Gulls are medium to large birds, but the size can vary depending on the species. Males tend to be larger than females. They have longish, sturdy bills and webbed feet. Gulls are mostly white or gray with light heads and gray wings and backs. They often have dark or striped patterns on the wings or tail. Juveniles are usually darker than adults and are mottled (spotted). They lighten slowly until they finally look like adults around age two. Check out the photos on the following pages to see some of the field marks (body differences) that can help you identify local gulls.

FOOD: More than any other coastal bird, gulls will truly eat anything they can find. If you watch them poke around tide pools and the wrack line, you can see these birds gobbling

Western gulls with a sea star snack and a couple of dangling mussels for dessert

down fish, small crabs, and even spiny sea stars. They'll steal food and eggs from other birds and animals. They'll dig through trash. They'll eat dead carcasses from the side of the road. And if you're not careful while snacking outdoors, they'll even swoop down and take your food as you're lifting it to your own mouth!

Who knew? Gulls don't steal food just from people—some are known for snatching fish from brown pelicans. They follow the pelicans around and grab any fish they can reach right out of the other bird's giant pouch.

HABITAT: Some type of gull can almost always be seen near the shore. Whether it's a sandy beach or a rocky inlet or even a sheer cliff rising out of the surf, there's a good chance you will see gulls.

REPRODUCTION: Gulls scrape a nest area out on the ground and line it with grasses and feathers. They lay from one to three eggs per clutch.

These birds nest in colonies, often with many other bird species, including cormorants. They return to the same location to breed year after year. Both the male and female gull take turns sitting on the nest to incubate the eggs (keep them warm). If it's really hot outside, the adult might fly down to the

water to get wet and then cool down the eggs with its wet body. Babies hatch with their eyes open and thick down all over their bodies (precocial). They're ready to explore nearby after just a couple of days.

RANGE: Found from Alaska down to the Gulf of California, Mexico (the California gull can be found the farthest south in Mexico).

Species to Look For

CALIFORNIA GULL *(Larus californicus)*

To identify a California gull, look for a medium-sized gull with a white head, dark eyes, and a gray back. Its legs and bill are yellow—those yellow legs are a good identifying mark—and there's a red spot on its lower beak. They have black tips on their wings, which fold back and cover their tail when they're walking or swimming. Juveniles are mottled brown

for their first two years and have pinkish legs and a pinkish bill with a black tip.

HEERMANN'S GULL *(Larus heermanni)*
Heermann's gulls were named after Adolphus Lewis Heermann, a doctor and naturalist back in the 1850s. They are some of the easiest gulls to identify because of their black-tipped bright red bill. They have dark gray wings and a lighter gray chest. On a breeding adult, the head is bright white, but on a juvenile or nonbreeding adult, the head is gray. Young

juveniles also don't have the red beak. These gulls come up the coast from June through September after they breed on rocky islands in the Gulf of California.

WESTERN GULL *(Larus occidentalis)*
This large gull is white with gray wings, a black back, and black wing tips. Its legs are pink, and its bill is yellow with a red spot near the lower tip. Their pink legs can help you tell them apart from California gulls. Juveniles are a soft, mottled brown instead of white and gray and have a black-ish bill. The western gull can be found from Baja California, Mexico, up to southern British Columbia.

Heron, Great Blue

(Ardea herodias)

This is another waterbird that might not spring to mind when you think of the beach. But great blue herons are frequently sighted all along the Pacific coast. These stately, beautiful birds are often staring into the water, motionlessly searching for their next meal. As you look at them, it's easy to see why scientists now say birds are descended from dinosaurs.

APPEARANCE: Great blue herons are another of the largest birds on the coast, right up there with bald eagles and brown pelicans. They can stand over 4 feet tall and have a 6-foot wingspan, but—incredibly—they weigh only about 5½ pounds! Great blue herons are really more gray than blue. They have a white head with a dark feathery swoosh over their eye on both sides. Males and females look alike.

FOOD: While you can often spot them fishing, great blue herons also hunt for other small critters to grab or stab with their long beak. They eat amphibians, small mammals, insects, and even small birds. You may find large herons standing in the water near the shore in a calm bay or inlet waiting to snatch small fish and invertebrates. You may also see one making use of its light body to stand on top of floating kelp to hunt for larger fish in deeper water.

HABITAT: Great blue herons are shorebirds that thrive around the bounty of seafood provided by the Pacific Ocean. They can also often be spotted roosting in trees near water.

REPRODUCTION: Since you mostly see great blue herons fishing, you might think their nest would be on the ground nearby. But great blue herons usually settle in the high branches of tall trees. They build huge nests (up to 4 feet across) out of sticks in colonies with a lot of other herons and sometimes even with other wading birds like egrets. Birders have found heronries with hundreds of nests in them, all clustered together in tree groves. The female great blue heron may lay between two and six large pale blue eggs. Babies hatch out covered in gray down, looking even more like dinosaurs than their parents.

RANGE: Great blue herons are found throughout most of North America and year-round from Alaska to Baja California, Mexico.

Murre, Common

(Uria aalge)

Look at the tops of rocky Pacific coast islands between April and September. Do you see a murre (rhymes with *sir*)? More precisely, do you see several thousand murres? These seabirds seem to blanket every rocky island along the coast during breeding season.

APPEARANCE: While they look a little like penguins, common murres are part of the auk (pronounced like *sock* without the *s*) family and are related to pigeon guillemots (see page 178) and puffins (see page 184). Murres are about the same size as a crow and have a blackish-brown face, head, back, and feet. Their underparts are bright white. They almost look like they're wearing a stretchy pullover hood and cape atop a white bodysuit.

FOOD: Common murres are fish eaters. That sometimes includes other tasty creatures that live alongside fish, such as squid and octopuses. The common murre is a deep-sea diver that uses its wings to "fly" underwater. In fact, it's a better swimmer than it is a flier (although it *can* fly). A murre catches and often eats its prey while diving. If it wants to keep fish in its mouth to take home for a baby or mate, the murre will press the fish against sharp spines (called denticles) on the roof of its mouth.

HABITAT: Murres are seabirds that often only come near shore to reproduce.

Common murre loomery

REPRODUCTION: Common murres nest on the bare rocks in super crowded colonies called loomeries—often with thirty or more birds per square meter! Picture a square on the ground that is about 3 feet long on each side. Then imagine thirty crow-sized birds inside, each trying to raise a baby. Whoa!

Maybe because it's so crowded, each female murre lays just one egg per year. The egg can range from pale tan to turquoise blue and splotchy. All murre eggs are very pointed at one end, so if the egg rolls it will just move in a circle. That's a lot better than rolling off a cliff or getting stepped on by someone's mom or dad! A

Common murre eggshell

few weeks after hatching—before it can even fly—the baby murre jumps into the water with a parent (usually the male). Going back to the nest isn't an option for the chick. The water is its new home as it grows. Good thing it's a great diver and swimmer right from the start!

RANGE: Found year-round from Alaska to Northern California and in Central (and occasionally Southern) California during the winter.

Juvenile common murre

Oystercatcher, Black

(Haematopus bachmani)

When you spot a black oystercatcher on the shore, you may also see its mate. These shorebird pairs stay together year-round, which isn't always the case in the birding world. If you don't spot oyster-catchers with your eyes, listen for their high-pitched whistling call as they fly nearby.

APPEARANCE: Black oystercatch-ers are a stunning sight. This bird is brownish black with a black head and light pink legs. It's a bit chunkier than a crow. Its vivid red bill is tipped in yellowish orange, almost glowing like a sunset. It also has red rings surrounding its yellow eyes.

Black oystercatcher with a limpet

FOOD: Oystercatchers eat lots of different mollusks, including mussels and limpets. Interestingly, they rarely eat oysters. Maybe "musselcatcher" or "limpetcatcher" just didn't sound right to early naturalists.

HABITAT: You can find black oystercatchers near mussel

Baby oystercatchers can run around and explore shortly after hatching. Good thing they blend in with the rocks so well!

beds and protected tide pool areas with limpets, chitons, and small crabs available for grazing.

REPRODUCTION: Oystercatchers will typically make their nest near where they forage for food. They make a scrape in the ground on a rocky or sandy beach above the high-water line. Often, they find nesting sites on the small islands that dot the Pacific coast. The little chick in the photo was hatched from a nest tucked into the base of Haystack Rock on the Oregon coast. Babies are precocial and can walk and explore as soon as they're dry after hatching.

RANGE: Found from Alaska down to Baja California, Mexico.

Pelican, Brown

(Pelecanus occidentalis)

Brown pelicans are huge seabirds that you can see flying together in straight lines or diving for food along the coast. They have a large bill with a giant stretchy throat pouch, a long neck that they tuck back while flying, and a wingspan of over 6 feet.

Who knew? Some people say that pelicans stick their spinal columns out through their mouths to cool themselves off. That would be a cool trick, but it turns out the real explanation for this behavior is much simpler (but still pretty wild to see): pelicans do this when they're stretching or yawning. The flexible pouch on their bill presses back against their throat and looks for all the world like the bird is turning inside out.

APPEARANCE: The brown pelican's appearance changes during breeding season and as it grows from juvenile to adult (which can take three to five years). Juveniles are grayish brown all over and have a dark gray bill. Adults have grayish-brown backs with white underparts and white necks with a golden crown at the top. They have short black legs and

Adult brown pelican

webbed feet. During breeding season, the back of the adult pelican's neck turns deep brown, and the throat pouch often turns a deep red.

FOOD: Brown pelicans mostly eat small fish, such as sardines and herrings, that live near the surface of the water. From the beach, you can watch these birds doing big splashy dives for their prey. With each dive, the pelican slams into little fish in the water below, stunning them so they can't move. It then scoops the dazed fish into its giant throat pouch along with about 2½ gallons of water. After the water drains out, the pelican can swallow its fish dinner. Sometimes pelicans will also grab bigger snacks as they're floating on the surface, including larger fish, shrimp, and other water creatures.

As brown pelicans dive into the water, they twist their neck to the left. Can you see it? That protects their airway and throat from the impact of the dive.

LOOK! PELICANS!

When you look out over the waves, you may see something wonderful that your parents or grandparents probably didn't see at your age: brown pelicans! Even just a few decades ago, you'd almost never see one along the Pacific coast—or anywhere else in North America. What changed? Back in the 1960s and '70s, humans figured out that one of the chemicals we were spraying on everything to kill pesky bugs was hurting birds. The chemical, called DDT, made their eggshells too thin to survive being sat on by bird parents. Lots of larger birds, from eagles to falcons to pelicans, were almost driven to extinction.

But instead of completely killing off some of our coolest birds, humans made changes. The United States banned DDT in 1972, and Canada mostly phased it out by the mid–1970s and stopped allowing it entirely by 1985. Conservationists worked hard to help pelicans repopulate the places they used to live. By 2009, brown pelicans were no longer an endangered species! Now there are over 140,000 brown pelicans living along the West Coast and about 370,000 worldwide. Every pelican you see is proof that working to help the natural world can have huge payoffs.

HABITAT: Brown pelicans live along the coast near shallow waters. You can see them just off the beach fishing or perched on rocks out in the surf. When they nest, brown pelicans will either choose a spot on the ground hidden by shrubs and grasses, or they'll make a nest up in a tree. Most nesting happens down south in warmer areas closer to the equator.

REPRODUCTION: The female lays one or two eggs in a single clutch once a year. Baby pelicans hatch after about a month and then spend an additional three months as nestlings (babies being cared for by their parents full-time).

RANGE: Brown pelicans can be found from southern British Columbia all the way down to South America along the Pacific coast, as well as over on the Atlantic shore. Many of the West Coast pelicans are migrants that breed down in the warmer climates from Baja California, Mexico, to about Ecuador in South America. Those pelicans often migrate north to British Columbia from June to mid-November before heading back south to breed. Other pelicans are year-round residents that you can spot even in the winter months in Southern California and further south.

While not really a Pacific coastal bird, you might see an American white pelican (*Pelecanus erythrorhynchos*), cousin of the brown pelican, near the beach in the summer. (This photo was taken on Whidbey Island in Washington in mid-August.) These large birds live mostly inland, where they rest on freshwater lakes and wetlands during migration. They are bright white with black flight feathers, a combination that makes them easy to tell apart from coastal brown pelicans.

Pigeon Guillemot

(Cepphus columba)

Look at those red feet! Doing a little marching dance to show off those ruby slippers is how male pigeon guillemots (pronounced PI-jun GILL-a-motts) attract their mates. If you look carefully, you'll notice the inside of their mouth matches their feet. This bird swims and dives a lot like a duck, but its sharp pointed bill indicates that it's definitely something else. A pigeon guillemot is a type of auk—a category of seabird that includes murres and puffins. They all look and act a little like penguins, except auks can fly. They're also excellent swimmers and divers.

APPEARANCE: The pigeon guillemot is a medium-sized seabird. It is very dark brown (almost black) with a splash of white over each wing. Its eyes and bill are black, while its legs, feet, and inside of its mouth are bright red.

FOOD: Pigeon guillemots eat fish as well as other ocean creatures

Pigeon guillemot with a fish for dinner

like worms, shrimp, and fish eggs. They dive under the surf and catch one fish at a time, often near the ocean floor in cracks or holes in rocks. Like many other seabirds, they have sharp points inside their bills that help hold the fish in their mouth once it's caught.

HABITAT: Pigeon guillemots live and hunt closer in to shore than many other seabirds. You can watch them dive for food if you pay attention—especially during nesting season in the summer! Look for their nest holes near the tops of rocky or sandy cliffs along the beach.

Can you spot the guano that marks this as a bird's nest? It's a pigeon guillemot burrow!

REPRODUCTION: Pigeon guillemots nest in rock crevices or burrows above the high-water line. Sometimes they dig their own burrows, but other times they use old holes dug by rabbits and other animals. Females lay one to two eggs per clutch.

RANGE: Found from Alaska down to Southern California.

Plover

Plover is one of those bird name pronunciations that birders like to disagree about. Some people, especially in Great Britain, pronounce *plover* so it rhymes with *lover*. Others, especially Americans, pronounce *plover* so it rhymes with *over*. Honestly? It doesn't really matter. Either way, they're great birds!

Semipalmated Plover
(Charadrius semipalmatus)

APPEARANCE: These plovers are fairly small. They can be up to about 7½ inches long and weigh under 2 ounces—less than a couple of AA batteries. They are brown on top and white underneath with yellow legs. Breeding adults have a black band across their breast. They have more black patches just above their orange beak—which has a black tip—and over the crown of their head, plus a white bar across their forehead. In nonbreeding adults, all the black parts are a duller brown.

FOOD: Plovers have a distinctive hunting style: they'll run a short way, then stop and look for prey. Then they'll run again. It's a lot like how a robin hunts in a grassy yard. These birds eat a variety of small prey such as shrimp, isopods, worms, clams, and mole crabs. Plovers and their eggs can be prey for gulls, foxes, raccoons, and rats.

HABITAT: These birds like to pick at the edges of water (oceans, bays, rivers, ponds) for their food. You may see them hunting along mudflats or sandbars near the ocean, and they'll roost at night right on the sandy beach.

REPRODUCTION: Semipalmated plovers nest in the Arctic (the far northern parts of Canada and Alaska) in shallow scrapes in the ground lined with rocks, shells, grass, and seaweed. The males and females share egg-sitting and chick-watching duties. The chicks are born ready to go as soon as they're dry.

RANGE: After breeding in the Arctic, these birds migrate to spend winters on the coast—in the west, that means from Oregon down to the coast of Peru in South America. They also migrate down the Atlantic coast. If you're up in Canada or Alaska, you can see them during the summer breeding months. During migration in the fall and early spring, this plover can be spotted throughout North America—even inland—since its migration crosses the entire continent.

Snowy Plover
(Charadrius nivosus)

APPEARANCE: Snowy plovers are chubby little shorebirds that have small black pointed bills and gray legs. They are only about 6 inches long and weigh less than 2 ounces. Snowy plovers are a pale sandy color on top (which is important for their habitat) with

white underparts. In the summer, breeding adult males have a black spot on their forehead and black swoops at their neck that don't circle all the way around. The female has those markings too, but in a softer brown instead of black.

Plover tracks can be fun to hunt for along the sand. You can tell them apart from other bird tracks by the crooked back toe. If you hold your right hand up with your first two fingers and thumb stretched out as far as they'll go, it looks a bit like a snowy plover track.

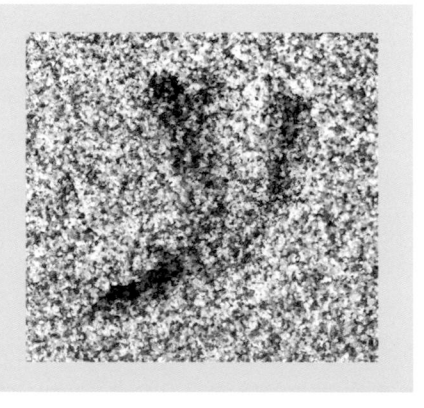

FOOD: These cute little shorebirds pick through the sand with their beaks to hunt for insects, worms, and small crustaceans. They run quickly to a new location and then stop to look around slowly for prey.

HABITAT: Snowy plovers live and forage mostly on dry sand near salt water. They even nest out in the open, which can be a problem. On the one hand, they're well camouflaged since their sandy coloring blends in well with their beach surroundings. On the other hand, beaches are full of other creatures—including dogs, horses, coyotes, raccoons, and humans—that can cause big problems for nesting birds. Conservation workers try to help by closing off parts of the beach to humans and their animals, bikes, and toys during summer breeding months. You can help by following all posted restrictions and watching your step.

REPRODUCTION: From March through September, snowy plovers lay from two to six sand-colored eggs in small depressions they scrape out of the dry sand well above the wrack line. The chicks are precocial and can leave the nest with their parents as soon as they're dry.

RANGE: Found from Washington down to Baja California, Mexico.

Who knew? Snowy plovers are considered threatened in the United States, so scientists are working to protect these little shorebirds. In the photo you can see that this bird has been banded around its ankles. That allows researchers to identify and keep track of the bird throughout its life. This plover is a male, and he was banded as a chick in 2020 in the Oregon Dunes National Recreation Area. This photo was taken in Nehalem, Oregon—about 160 miles away—in the summer of 2022.

Puffin, Tufted
(Fratercula cirrhata)

This beautiful bird is sometimes called a sea parrot because of the bright colors it shows off during breeding season. It is part of the auk family, which includes murres and guillemots.

APPEARANCE: These birds are about the size of a crow, but stockier and with shorter wings. They can fly—looking like footballs with their legs sticking out behind—but they are much better at swimming. While floating out on the open sea, the puffin is dark all over with a dull-orange-and-gray bill. But when it's time to go ashore to find a mate and reproduce, it's like Cinderella getting ready for the ball. Tufted puffins grow white feathers on their face and long sweeping yellowish plumes (their tufts) on either side of their head. Even their bill grows and changes color until it's impressively huge and red-orange.

Look for a flying football to spot a tufted puffin in the sky.

FOOD: Tufted puffins eat fish. Their bills are specially designed with ridges that allow them to line up many little fish crossways without dropping any. Most of the year, these birds just eat underwater while they're hunting, sometimes over 300 feet deep. But during breeding season, they grab mouthfuls of fish to bring back to their chicks.

HABITAT: These are true seabirds. They live out on the open ocean, only coming back to land when they're ready to have babies. That means most tufted puffins spend the first three years of their lives (while they're growing to adulthood) never once going to shore! When they're ready to reproduce, they join colonies on the cliffs of rugged islands just off the coast. They dig burrows in the soil at the top of the cliff, often hidden by grasses and bushes.

REPRODUCTION: Tufted puffins lay one egg, which both parents take turns incubating. The chick that hatches is called a puffling—maybe the cutest baby name in the animal kingdom. It is ready to leave the nest after about a month and a half. Then the whole family goes back to sea.

RANGE: Tufted puffins live out in the ocean from Alaska down to Southern California. They are much more common in Alaska and off the coast of British Columbia than they are in Washington, Oregon, or California, but there are places to see them during breeding season in all three lower states.

> **Who knew?** Even though it has fewer puffins than its northern neighbors, Oregon has one of the only places in the continental United States where you can actually see tufted puffins without getting on a boat! Haystack Rock hosts a colony of these fascinating birds from April through July every year. Bring binoculars, because they nest near the top of the rock, and look for the friendly volunteers in red coats to help you spot your first puffin.

Doesn't this horned puffin (*Fratercula corniculata*) look like a stuffed animal? It's real, though. If you're lucky, you may spot one way out on the water or mixed in with a colony of tufted puffins in the springtime. If you want to see these gorgeous birds up close in the wild, you'll need to visit Alaska.

Sandpiper

Sandpipers are smallish wading birds with long, narrow bills. Beachgoers like to watch them running up and down the sand near the water. Sandpiper species can be hard to tell apart, so birders often just call them peeps, like the yellow marshmallow birds at the grocery store.

Least Sandpiper
(Calidris minutilla)

APPEARANCE: This is the world's smallest shorebird and is found all along the coast. They are between 5 and 6 inches long and weigh about the same as a slice of bread (1 ounce). They have brown speckled upperparts and white underparts. You can tell this sandpiper from its cousins by its greenish-yellow legs. Since they're waders, you may have to really look to see the color through the mud.

FOOD: Least sandpipers forage for insects and small invertebrates such as amphipods and isopods.

HABITAT: During migration, you can see least sandpipers on coastal mudflats and protected areas with small rocks. They peck around in the mud near water looking for food.

REPRODUCTION: Least sandpipers make tiny nests in grass and other vegetation on the ground. The nest is usually only 2 inches across. The sandpipers lay three to four eggs per clutch.

RANGE: These little peeps breed in northern Canada and Alaska in the summer, then fly to southern Oregon, California, Central America, and South America for the winter. The best time to see them in the Pacific Northwest is during spring and fall migrations.

Sanderling
(Calidris alba)

If you see a flock of tiny shorebirds running from the waves on the beach, more often than not those are sanderlings. These little birds are in the sandpiper family, but this species gets its own name.

Sanderling hunting

APPEARANCE: Sanderlings are darker and more rusty colored in the Arctic during their breeding season. But from British Columbia down through California, they are pale gray and white, with black bills and legs. They can be 7 to 8 inches long and weigh only

Sanderlings snacking at the waterline

about 3 ounces. Like many coastal birds, male and female sanderlings look alike.

FOOD: Sanderlings eat small creatures that live in sand along the water's edge. This includes mole crabs, marine worms, amphipods, and small crustaceans. They'll also sometimes nibble on plants and seaweed.

Sanderling and marine worm

HABITAT: You'll find sanderlings, like their name suggests, along sandy beaches near the waves. Look for them in the fall and winter.

REPRODUCTION: Sanderlings nest on the ground way up north in the Arctic, usually near a freshwater lake. Females will have one clutch of three to four eggs per year.

RANGE: When they aren't nesting, this species can be found all over the world—on every continent except Antarctica. They are one of the most widespread shorebirds, with some traveling over 6,000 miles from their breeding site to their off-season homes.

Western Sandpiper
(Calidris mauri)

APPEARANCE: This sandpiper is more colorful than the rest of the peeps in North America. During breeding season, it has rufous (reddish-brown), black, and brown

patterning on its upperparts. It also has rufous streaking on its crown (top of its head) and cheeks. Its underparts are white with brown streaks. Like the sanderling, its legs and bill are black. These birds are usually between 5½ and 6½ inches long and weigh about 1½ ounces.

FOOD: Western sandpipers eat small prey, including marine worms, small clams, amphipods, and isopods. They (and other peeps) also eat something called biofilm. Biofilm is a scummy layer in the water made up of microscopic organisms and tiny decaying pieces of living matter. When biofilm gets shaken up by a storm, it becomes sea foam.

HABITAT: You may see large flocks of western sandpipers, often with other peeps and shorebirds, on mudflats and sandy or rocky beaches.

REPRODUCTION: Western sandpipers make a small nest (about 2½ inches across) on the ground up on the tundra in Alaska. The female sandpiper lays between two and four eggs in a single clutch per year. Babies are active (precocial) and following their mom and dad out of the nest as soon as they're dry.

RANGE: These sandpipers mostly breed up in Alaska, but they can be found at other times of the year all along the Pacific coast down to the middle of South America. It is common to see them along the coast of Oregon, Washington, and British Columbia during spring and fall migrations.

Surf Scoter

(Melanitta perspicillata)

This cool bird is a type of sea duck you're most likely to spot out on the waves rather than on land, often in a giant flock.

APPEARANCE: Unlike a lot of seabirds, surf scoter males and females look different. Males are black with white eyes and have bright white patches on their forehead and the nape of their neck. They also have a large bill that looks orange from a distance but is actually a combination of orange, yellow, red, and white with a pair of large black spots at the base. Even from a distance, you can see the male surf scoter's huge bill.

The female surf scoter is mostly brown. Her bill is still pretty large, but it's dark gray and smaller than the male's. She has white patches on her cheeks and just behind each eye. Surf scoters of both sexes have pink legs and feet.

FOOD: These ducks are divers who eat small crabs, snails, clams, mussels, and marine worms. They hunt near breaking waves to take advantage of the ocean's power. When the waves crash and dislodge critters from the seafloor, the surf scoter is there to snatch them up. Surf scoters swallow their prey whole—even things with hard shells, such as clams and mussels. Birds have a second muscular stomach called a gizzard that they use to grind up their food instead of chewing. Many birds swallow small stones to help with this process, but surf scoters' gizzards just crush the shells they swallow and then use those to grind up the edible parts of the prey.

> **Who knew?** Like several other seabirds, surf scoters have adaptations to let them live in and around so much salt water. They have special glands up above their eyes that remove extra salt from their diet. The salt just drips harmlessly out of their nostrils. The salt glands get bigger when the surf scoter is out to sea in the winter and shrink when the birds fly up to their inland freshwater breeding grounds in the summer.

HABITAT: Look for surf scoters in large flocks out near the breaking waves. They'll ride the waves and then quickly dive down when one starts to break.

REPRODUCTION: These birds build nests on the ground in northern Canada and Alaska. The female lays up to nine eggs per clutch, and she is the one who incubates them and teaches the chicks to hunt. Chicks hatch covered in down and ready to follow mom as soon as they're dry.

RANGE: Surf scoters breed up in central northern Canada and Alaska in the summer, but you can find them during the winter from Alaska to Baja California, Mexico.

Tern, Caspian

(Hydroprogne caspia)

This tern gets its name because it was first observed near the Caspian Sea, which is between Europe and Asia. It can also be found across North America.

APPEARANCE: The Caspian tern looks a bit like a gull, but with a longer and differently shaped bill. Terns are white with silvery-gray upper wings and a black cap. They also have a noticeable bright red pointed bill.

FOOD: This bird will fly over the water with its bill pointing down looking for fish. When it spies some prey, it dives out of the air to catch the fish just below the surface.

HABITAT: These fish eaters need to be near water, either fresh or salt. They can often be spotted roosting in large flocks mixed in with gulls and other coastal birds.

Terns will often hover for a bit before they dive for their prey.

REPRODUCTION: Terns build nests on the ground that are ringed with pebbles and shells and lined with dried grasses and plants. The female lays up to three eggs, which hatch covered in down. Chicks are able to leave the nest after just a few days.

RANGE: This species can be found along the Pacific coast during fall and spring migrations. There are even some summer breeding grounds scattered through southern Canada, Washington, and Oregon. Their full range covers wide swaths of North America.

Who knew? The largest breeding colony of Caspian terns in the world is in the Pacific Northwest on East Sand Island in the mouth of the Columbia River between Oregon and Washington. They share the 62–acre island with a huge breeding colony of double-crested cormorants as well as various gulls and brown pelicans.

Turnstone, Black
(Arenaria melanocephala)

As their common name implies, turnstones turn over stones and piles of detritus (dead stuff) washed up along the wrack line as they search for food. Sightings along the coast south of Alaska will be of their less contrasting and colorful nonbreeding plumage.

APPEARANCE: Turnstones are about the size of a robin—just under about 10 inches long—but stockier. During the nonbreeding season, the black turnstone is actually more brown than black. It has a bright white belly and two white stripes on each wing that you can see when it flies.

You may also come across a more rusty-colored turnstone with brighter orange legs called the ruddy turnstone (*Arenaria interpres*).

FOOD: Black turnstones eat a wide variety of aquatic invertebrates, including isopods, amphipods, limpets, and marine worms. They'll also eat dead fish and various insects when available.

HABITAT: These wading birds can be found foraging on rocky beaches and jetties. You can also sometimes find them searching for food on mudflats or roosting on rocky cliffs above the high-water line.

Who knew? Sometimes you can spot black turnstones standing on the vertical side of a cliff looking for isopods on the stones instead of turning them over on the ground. It certainly helps to be light and able to fly if there's a misstep!

REPRODUCTION: Black turnstones scrape out nests on the ground among rushes (like long grasses with round stems) up in western Alaska. They lay up to four eggs in a clutch. The chicks hatch covered in down and ready to leave the nest soon after they dry.

RANGE: These turnstones are much more local than their widespread ruddy cousins. They breed up in Alaska and then make their way down the coast as far south as the Gulf of California, Mexico, throughout the winter.

Wandering Tattler

(Tringa incana)

There's a type of bird with the same name as someone who tells on a naughty kid! In this case, though, the tattler alerts all the other birds that a hunter is on the prowl. It's called a wandering tattler because it wanders far from its breeding grounds—sometimes to islands over 7,500 miles away in the South Pacific. Even though this is technically in the sandpiper family (see page 187), it is different enough that it's usually considered separately. Some naturalists, including famous bird expert David Allen Sibley, think of these as "rock-pipers" instead.

APPEARANCE: When you first notice a wandering tattler, you may realize that you've been overlooking it for years because it is so well camouflaged. They are gray on top and light below, with a dark bill and yellow legs. Look for their legs to spot them on gray rocks. This is a medium-sized shorebird, reaching about 11 inches long with a 20-inch wingspan.

FOOD: Wandering tattlers eat insects and small invertebrates like isopods and amphipods. You can see them poking around large rocks or sea stacks. They also run up and down the beach with the waves like a sanderling (see page 188).

HABITAT: Wandering tattlers prefer rocky intertidal zones, including places like reefs and manmade jetties.

REPRODUCTION: These birds nest on the ground near streams up on the tundra in northern Canada and Alaska. The female lays three to four eggs, and both parents share incubation duties. Chicks hatch covered in down and ready to follow their parents out of the nest as soon as they're dry.

RANGE: Tattlers breed up in northern Canada and Alaska. In the winter, they wander all the way down past South America. Some have even traveled as far as Australia!

A wandering tattler fluttering down from a rock covered with sea life in the intertidal zone.

Whimbrel

(Numenius phaeopus)

Check out the bill on this bird!

APPEARANCE: This is a large shorebird with a long, downturned bill. Its body can be up to 18 inches long with a wingspan of around 32 inches. Its feathers are streaked brown and tan, and it has a dark crown with a grayish stripe in the center and a dark stripe through each eye.

FOOD: Whimbrels eat small crabs, mole crabs, marine worms, sea cucumbers, sand shrimp, and other invertebrates living in the intertidal zone. They also commonly eat berries, insects, and spiders.

HABITAT: Whimbrels live near and hunt on mudflats, oyster beds, reefs, and salt marshes. In areas developed for human use, you may also spot

them foraging on large grassy areas such as golf courses (as in the photo on page 199).

REPRODUCTION: Female whimbrels lay between two and four eggs in a nest on high ground that has been lined with leaves, grasses, and lichen. The chicks hatch covered in down and ready to leave the nest almost immediately.

RANGE: Whimbrels breed up in the Arctic and then can be seen along the Pacific coast during fall and spring migrations. During the winter months, they are found from central Oregon down to South America.

Acknowledgments

A huge, Pacific-sized thank-you to everyone who helped and encouraged me as I created this guide. Michelle McCann brainstormed beach creatures with me and brought the idea to the team at Sasquatch Books. Christy Cox and all the editors, designers, and staff at Little Bigfoot polished my words and photos until they gleamed. Austin and Caden helped me translate complex science into kid-speak without losing the essence. Dad gave me a place to sleep between nudibranch and puffin safaris. Mom took me to the beach all through my formative years and beyond. Aunt Linda and Uncle Jamie gave me access to the tide pools and rock formations of the central Oregon coast. Angel drove hours with me to explore beach life in northwestern Washington. Jesse helped me spot barnacle cirri and shiny blue mussel worms. Lori and Richmond were awesome hand models. My other friends (and several beachgoing strangers) listened and humored me as I talked through the mind-boggling richness of life along the shore. Thank you to the amazing volunteers at Haystack Rock, Larrabee State Park, and the Seattle Aquarium, as well as to bird guide Allison from Portland Audubon, Marie at Tillamook Bait Company, and Angela from NCLC. My wonderful husband, Eric, continues to be my biggest help and most devoted fan. He schlepped my camera gear up and down countless trails to explore low tides with me in the predawn. Without him, none of this would have been possible.

Finally, I dedicate this book in loving memory of my brother, Jason, who would have delighted in every page.

Glossary

ADAPTATION: A physical feature or behavior that helps an animal survive in a particular environment.

ALTRICIAL: Born helpless and requiring lots of parental care.

ARISTOTLE'S LANTERN: The star-shaped mouth on the underside of a sea urchin.

BIOFILM: A layer of bacteria and microorganisms.

BIOLUMINESCENCE: Light emitted by biological organisms such as phytoplankton and sea jellies.

BIVALVE: A mollusk, such as a clam or a mussel, that has a hinged shell with two halves.

BLADE: The part of a seaweed that is like a leaf on a land plant.

BUDDING: A method of reproduction where an organism grows a small version of itself that breaks off and becomes a new individual.

BUOYANT: Able to stay afloat.

BYSSUS: The threads mussels produce to stick themselves to rocks and each other.

CAMOUFLAGE: Using colors and patterns to help blend into the surroundings.

CARAPACE: The hard upper shell of a crustacean such as a crab.

CARNIVORE: A meat eater.

CASTING: The sand or mud waste that is passed by a worm after going through its body.

CENTRAL DISC: The middle of a sea star that isn't part of the legs.

CERATA: Wavy body structures found on the upper surfaces of aeolid nudibranchs.

CHLOROPHYLL: A green pigment that plants and algae use to make their own food through photosynthesis.

CIRRI: The feathery legs of a barnacle.

CLONE: An organism formed from another organism that is genetically identical; a copy.

CLUTCH: A group of eggs hatched together.

CNIDARIA: A big biological group of soft-bodied stinging animals such as sea jellies and anemones.

CRUSTACEAN: An animal with a segmented body, hard exoskeleton, jointed legs, antennae, and gills.

DECAPOD: A type of crustacean with ten legs on its thorax.

DETRITUS: Organic matter produced when organisms decompose.

ECHINODERM: An invertebrate marine mammal with a hard, spiny covering or skin.

EXOSKELETON: A hard outer layer that protects and supports an animal's body.

FLOAT: On seaweed, an air-filled pouch that keeps the blades near the water's surface to collect sunlight.

GASTROPOD: A group of mollusks including snails, slugs, and limpets.

GILL: An organ that allows marine creatures to extract oxygen from the water (breathe).

GIRDLE: The fleshy band that holds together the separate shells of a chiton.

GUANO: Bird poop (this term is also used for the poop of reptiles and bats).

HERBIVORE: A plant eater.

HOLDFAST: The part of a seaweed that grabs on to rocks or the seafloor.

INVERTEBRATE: An animal that doesn't have a backbone.

KEYSTONE SPECIES: A species that is so important to an ecosystem that removing it would change the environment drastically.

KING TIDE: An extra high tide that can occur during a new or full moon.

LARVA: The immature form of a creature such as insects and many sea creatures.

MADREPORITE: The valve that controls the seawater system of an echinoderm, such as a sea star.

MARINE: Found in the sea.

MICROSCOPIC: So small you need a microscope to see it.

MINUS TIDE: A tide that is farther out than the usual lowest tide at a particular location.

MOLLUSK: An invertebrate from a large group of soft, unsegmented animals including snails, clams, squid, and octopuses.

MOLT: When an animal sheds its shell, feathers, or skin to make way for new growth. The word is used both for the action (to molt) and for the old, cast-off outer layer (such as a crab shell).

NATURALIST: An expert or student of nature.

NEMATOCYST: Stinger cells in the tentacles of a sea jelly, anemone, or similar creatures used for defense.

OPALESCENT: Reflecting light in a rainbow of colors.

OPERCULUM: The hard plate that seals a snail into its shell to protect it from predators and keep it from drying out.

ORAL ARMS: On a true sea jelly, these are the long structures that surround the mouth and bring food toward it.

PEDUNCLE: The rubbery stalk that connects a gooseneck barnacle to a rock.

PEEP: A general name for any of about a dozen species of small sandpipers.

PHOTOSYNTHESIS: The process by which green plants and algae use sunlight to create food from carbon dioxide and water.

PHYTOPLANKTON: Microscopic free-floating plants and algae in seawater.

PINNIPED: An aquatic mammal such as a seal or sea lion.

PLEOPOD: The swimming limb of a crustacean; also called a swimmeret.

PLUMAGE: A bird's feathers.

POLYP: An invertebrate animal, such as a sea anemone or coral, that is attached to a surface. The body is often tube-shaped with tentacles on one end.

PRECOCIAL: Hatched or born able to move around and fend for itself almost immediately.

PROBOSCIS: In worms, an extendable tube-shaped sucking organ.

RADULA: A mollusk's tongue-like structure that is covered in microscopic sharp teeth and used for scraping and feeding.

RAY: The arm of a sea star (starfish).

RHINOPHORE: One of two tentacle-like structures on the back of the head of a nudibranch (sea slug) that allow it to "smell" (detect) chemicals in the water.

ROOKERY: A breeding colony of birds or seals.

ROOST: A verb describing birds sleeping for the night—also a noun describing *where* they sleep. Birds roost on a roost.

SCAVENGER: Animals that eat dead plants and animals.

SEMIAQUATIC: An organism that spends time both in the water and on land.

SIPHON: A tube in the body of an aquatic animal that draws in or expels water.

SPAWN: As a verb, to release or deposit eggs. As a noun, it describe the eggs themselves, such as a sea urchin releasing its spawn (eggs) into the surf.

SPRAY ZONE: The area just above the top of the intertidal zone that often gets splashed but not covered in water.

STIPE: A seaweed stalk.

SUSPENSION FEEDER: An animal that filters floating food out of the water for its nutrition.

SWASH ZONE: The part of a beach where waves run up the sand.

TENTACLE: A thin, flexible body part used for grasping or feeling (sensing), especially around the mouth of an invertebrate.

TEST: The hard shell of a rounded marine creature such as an anemone or sand dollar.

TRANSLUCENT: Allows light to pass through.

TRANSPARENT: Completely see-through.

TUNIC: The shared or individual outer coat of a tunicate (sea pork or sea squirt).

UMBO: The highest point (bump) on each half of a bivalve shell.

WRACK LINE: The line on the beach where debris is left at high tide.

ZOOPLANKTON: Plankton that are animals—especially the larvae and eggs of various sea creatures.

Index

Answers to What Do You See (pages 98-99):

1 Giant acorn barnacles
2 Gooseneck barnacles
3 Limpets (hiding in the gooseneck barnacles)
4 Ochre sea stars
5 Chiton (just below the number)

6 California mussels
7 Giant green anemones
8 Aggregating anemones
9 Pacific blue mussels

Hidden limpets in the Who Knew (page 48)

About the Author

Karen DeWitz is an unapologetically enthu-
siastic nature nerd. She loves nothing better
than to grab her camera and head outside to
explore, delighting in the sometimes well-
hidden discoveries to be made along the way.
Karen has a rich background in instruction,
outdoor education, and photography. As
a former teacher with a master's degree in
education, she understands how to intrigue
and inspire young people. She has experience
both in the classroom and in Northwest wild
places—teaching, writing, exploring, and mar-
veling in the beauty of the Pacific Northwest.